From Heaven to Earth: Soft Landing Your Family Budget

From Heaven to Earth: Soft Landing Your Family Budget

14 steps to manage downsizing family finances in downsizing times

Michelle Eagles

Writers Club Press
New York Lincoln Shanghai

From Heaven to Earth: Soft Landing Your Family Budget
14 steps to manage downsizing family finances in downsizing times

Writers Club Press
an imprint of iUniverse, Inc.

For information address:
iUniverse
2021 Pine Lake Road, Suite 100
Lincoln, NE 68512
www.iuniverse.com

For question about rights and permissions contact:

Galiel.Net
704 228th Ave. NE, # 173
Sammamish, WA 98074-7222
http://www.Galiel.Net
Michelle@Galiel.Net

ISBN: 0-595-25916-2 (Pbk)
ISBN: 0-595-65431-2 (Cloth)

Printed in the United States of America

14 Steps to Handle Downsizing family Budget

Content

Introduction: How to read and use this book

Who is this book for?

In 1999, according to IRS data, my family got into the first 5% of American households by income. Surprisingly, we were not rich, we still were uncomfortable about the time, our kids will go to a college, and our retirement plans were far from clear, but it was not too bad either. We were able to have what we need, keep accounting loose, and the balance on the checking account was still slowly, but persistently coming up. In 2001, with dot-Com melt, my company downsized and I had lost my job as a software developer. We started to live on my husband's salary and every month became a struggle. Sounds familiar?

Today many families find themselves in a complicated financial situation. Families, who lived on two salaries, have to adjust to only one. Families, who counted on stock options, now have to live on salary. And salaries don't grow today as they used to, if they grow at all. Despite all the money you still bring home, and all the efforts you apply, you are still slowly, but consistently going down. These are the families, this book is written for.

You may be in a higher or lower income than I was, but with a smaller income, you face the same problems, I did, and the same challenges, I faced. You need to transition from a loose accounting to a strong grip on your family finances. You need to cut or decrease some expenses. You need to find some new sources for income. This is what this book is about.

If you have no income at all, high mortgage payments, credit for a new car, and expensive habits all at the same time, this book is unlikely to help you. Even if you don't have expensive habits, but no income whatsoever, there is not much any advice could do. That's just that simple: to spend money you need to have money, to have money you have to earn money. At least I have never heard of a magic, which would bring money without a work.

But if you have a job, and still scramble your way through life with your checking account balance going down every month, then this book is for you. Even if it does not go down, but it does not going up either, and you are scared when you think how to send kids to a college or where to get money to buy a car, when the one, you have now, will break down, then this book is for you.

Survival in downsizing economy is not fun. It's not easy to keep flying when everything else is falling. But it's possible and must be done, because you have no other options.

And about fun, you may be surprised, how much money you are spending on the stuff, which is actually taking fun out of your life.

How to read this book

The book consists of several chapters describing the steps you need to take, one after another. Unless you do at least something on one step, there is usually not much point in moving into another. You may also consider this book as a series of hints. Try one, get the result, and if it's not enough, then go to the next one.

If you will prefer just to read this book from cover to cover, it still will bring you good insights and sound ideas, how to handle your finances.

It's just that doing usually beats thinking, at least if thinking is all you do. Therefore our advice would be to actually do the suggested work, not leave it for later. This book was written so compact on purpose. We don't want you waste your time on *reading*, when you can spend it actually *doing*.

Some steps will not bring you immediate relief, but instead they will bring you a better knowledge of what's going on. Such are most of the initial steps. You still need to do them, because they tell you what to do on the following steps.

On this note, dear fellow American, let's dive in and change our lives for the better!

Step-1: Your Family

Get Commitment from your Family

Yes, this is not a mistake. This is the step minus one. That is the step, which you should make before doing anything else, even step zero. And here is why…

Before you can do anything, you need to talk to your spouse, a.k.a. wife, husband, significant other, or whatever way you prefer to call him or her. In fact, you need a commitment from anybody with whom you share your income, expenses, and accounts, also known as *money*. That can include your parents, grandparents, brothers, sisters, children, and their families. However several generations under the same roof are extremely rare in the United States. And besides, the people who are tough enough to live with their grandparents almost never get into financial trouble. You actually don't even have to live under the same roof. It's enough if you can get under the same roof to survive hard times.

Anyway, this is rare, so most likely there is only one person, with whom you need to get on the terms to handle your finances. Why is this so important? The answer is simple. No matter how hard you try, this person can ruin all your efforts in a moment, and you will not be able to do anything about it. And at the same time, he or she may be your greatest ally in getting the things under control, while you will be the risk factor.

This is truly the very basic condition of managing your finances. Your loved one must at least abide to the rules you put for yourselves together, or ideally, work together with you on overcoming the problems.

Golden rule: Love

There is an even more basic rule: love. It sounds extraneous to such a book, but think for yourself, and you will see many reasons why love is very important for your own finances.

What is the reason why you want to be financially successful? To have fun, to enjoy quality of life, to send kids to college, to save for retirement…Whatever you are going to do, you are going to do that together. Whatever benefits will be, you will get them together. Whatever spoils or punishments await you on this road, it awaits both of you.

There is an old parable about a man, to whom God promised anything he could imagine, just for asking. There was only one condition: whatever the man gets, his neighbor gets twice more. The man said, "Take one of my eyes out." You see, it's very hard to work toward a goal, which you don't really want. You need to enjoy everything good which happens to your family, because that's what you will work toward. And to enjoy that, you need love, the real one. You must love your family, because they are the ones who will benefit most from your efforts.

And if you don't, or, God forbid, you hate the person with whom you share home, bed, and money, that's too bad. As you can see from the parable above, hate is very expensive. You just cannot afford it, even though money is the least thing you pay for the folly of hate.

Beside that, there is a lot more benefits of love, and reasons to avoid hate. Some of them will be mentioned below, when appropriate. Others just won't fit into the book of personal finances, but they still exist.

Step 0: If you have credit card debt...

"Credit card" is a deceitful name

It actually combines two: "credit" and "card". You should be very careful about which part of this name you are really using. Here is why. Let see what each part of the name means.

"Credit", a.k.a. "expensive long-term credit with instant access."

The first part, "credit", actually means "expensive long-term credit with instant access." If you'll look at it, each word in this definition means something bad for you.

"Expensive" means that you pay much more than you would pay if using alternative methods. Usual 17-20% APR rate on credit cards is way more expensive than 6-9% mortgages or 7-12% auto loans. For example, $10000 debt on a 20% credit card will consume more than $2000 in interest per year. Same debt on 12% auto loan will cost you $1200, and as a part of 7% mortgage it will cost you about $700. As you see, the difference is more than a thousand dollars in after-tax money. That hurts.

"Long-term" does not mean that creditors are kind and patient with you. That means that you pay it year after the year. It's bad enough that you have to waste your money on interest to service your debt, it really hurts when it continues long-term.

And "instant access" is a real killer. That does not mean "convenience", as credit card offers are trying to convince you. That means that it is damn easy to get into this expensive long-term debt, if you don't think what you are doing, each time you are getting this piece of plastic out of your wallet.

This is the reason why "credit" part of a credit card is what you should never or almost never use.

"Card", a.k.a. "payment card with a free short-term credit."

What about the second part, the "card"? It actually means "payment card with a free short-term credit."

As a payment card, it is as good and convenient as ATM or Check card, and it's accepted in a lot more places. It also means that you always get a receipt and a detailed monthly statement. If you have a computer then for most cards you can view all your transactions online or download them. That's a lot of accounting you would not get with a cash. And this information really helps, when you are trying to control your expenses.

"Free short-term credit" means that if you pay monthly in full within the grace period, the credit is free. There is no interest whatsoever. You just need to spend only what you can pay for and pay in time.

Is there a downside for this part of credit cards? Yes, there is. It's too close to the "credit" part. It's too easy to slip into the debt, if you are not careful and not adjusted to spend wisely.

"No credit" rule

Now it comes as no surprise that what you really need to avoid is the "credit" part. If you have credit card debt, get out of it, replace it with some more reasonable debt, or better try to eliminate it at all.

This is why we called this chapter "Step 0." It's really something you need to start from. That does not mean that you cannot proceed before you eliminate credit card debt, but you need to start to work on it.

Also you need to observe yourself and decide, if are you a kind of person, who can safely have a credit card in a pocket? Will you have enough control over yourself and common sense to never get yourself into a credit card debt? Many people are, but some are not. Ask yourself the same question about your family. Remember, they can get your whole family in the trouble as easily as you can.

People who cannot stand this piece of plastic in their hands just should not have it. Period. If they feel offended that they don't have one while somebody else in the family does, you need to handle that. If you cannot handle their emotional response, just eliminate all credit cards in the house. Yes, they are convenient, and they are great in emergency, and there are many more reasons, why credit cards are good, but all of them are not worth getting into the debt.

Exception from the "no credit" rule—0% APR introductory offers

There is one case, when you may want to break "no credit" rule. That's introductory offers. Usually you are getting such offers in the mail. They offer you to get a new "pre-approved" credit card with some introductory rate. Introductory means that it will not last forever, but just for a few months. Or, sometimes, your current credit cards may send you a convenience check with lower rate. Such rate may be also "introductory", that is for certain period of time. Or it may be until you will pay it off, but in this case it's normally higher.

Even if it's just few months, this is the time to handle other issues and get better financially. And if an introductory rate is better, than what you will get from the bank on a personal or any other loan, why not?

Of course, free cheese is found only in mousetraps, and that looks a lot like free cheese. So what's the catch? Here are the things you need to look for.

What is the rate?

Look at the rate, yes, the actual number they offer. If it's saying "As low as 9.99% APR!!!", throw the offer away without even reading. 9.99% *is not a great rate.*

Ideally, see for 0% APR. Yes, that's possible and that happens. You may wonder how the banks with such offers, are making money on them? It's simple. Everything we will tell below is used by banks to make money on such offers. So let's consider it in details, and make sure that they will not make money off you.

Is there a balance transfer fee?

Balance transfer often involves "balance transfer fee." It's especially likely, if you are using a convenience check or some other balance transfer option with an existing card. It is important to understand that such a fee effectively replaces an interest. The only difference is that you are paying it upfront, not accumulating it slowly.

Let consider an example. Suppose you are offered 4 months at 0%, but balance transfer fee is 3%. That effectively means that you are getting 8.58% APR without a fee, and that's not the best rate. See for yourself:

	0% APR and 3% Fee	8.58% APR and 0% Fee
Original amount	$1,000.00	$1,000.00
After the 1st month	$1,030.00	$1,007.41
After the 2nd month	$1,030.00	$1,014.88
After the 3rd month	$1,030.00	$1,022.41
After the 4th month	$1,030.00	$1,029.99

How long introductory period lasts?

Introductory period is usually indicated by the end date like "Until January 2003." Check if it's long enough and worth the trouble. After you will send an application, it will take several weeks until your card arrives and another month until the first statement. Effectively, if it's just two months from current date, you have a chance to get high rate already on the first statement. And that's not what you are planning, right?

Also keep in mind, that it will take some time to make the balance transfer, and some time to pay it out one way or another. It may be just not worth the trouble.

Are there any other fees?

Banks are very creative in inventing and naming some fees. The simplest one is annual fee. How about a statement fee? Some banks already do that for checking accounts.

Remember, it does not matter what's the formal reason and how it's called, it's what you pay that counts. Any fee decreases efficiency of the balance transfer. You need to be conscious of that and always look at the bottom line.

What's the rate afterward?

If we would not list this here, some readers would probably complain that we missed the "so important question." The truth is that this question is not important. You just don't want to have balance when the introductory rate is over.

Of course it's always prudent to check all conditions, but it's most likely that you will not like this one. The whole idea of this transaction is to avoid regular rate.

Other pitfalls to avoid

Besides carefully planted straightforward traps, as described above, there are plenty of opportunities to screw up afterward. So here are the points to look for:

- Plan to pay the balance off before introductory rate ends. Whether by cash, or by moving it into another form of credit. Seriously plan that, screw-ups may be expensive.

- Don't use the credit card until the balance is paid off. Interest on purchases will be incurred, because your monthly payments will be first applied to "0% APR" balance, and only after that to standard rate purchases. So if you will use the credit card, the new balance will be subject to interest until you will pay off "free" credit completely.

- After the introductory rate ends and the balance has been paid out, this is just another credit card. If you used it for credit once, it does not mean that it can be used for the same purpose again.

Overall, 0% APR is a good thing, if you need a short breath time, but don't overestimate it. That's just a temporary solution. Unless you get a permanent one, it will not save you.

Kinds of credit cards and credit card issuers

Though it's not so important for the main ideas of this chapter, let's get into a few details about the credit card business, what is good and what is bad there. First of all, there are three kinds of credit card issuers based on how they extract income from their operations:

- Creditors
- Servicing customers
- Servicing merchants

Creditors

These banks rely mostly on customers who carry balance and pay interest. Generally, every credit card issuer wants you to carry balance and pay interest. Yes, *every*. It's just that for some of them this is a primary goal in their business model, while other tend to consider alternatives as well.

Credit card companies of this category can be identified by their persistent attempts to get you signed off and eventually in debt to them. These are usurers in a classic fashion, who get American scale and magnitude.

Notice that both the Bible and the Koran prohibits usurers as a business, as well as dealing with them. No matter what your religious beliefs are, you'd better keep on this advice.

It's not a big surprise that these are the ones, who are most insistent on "introductory offers." That's probably the only exception of the rule of not dealing with them.

Servicing customers

This category derives most of their income from various "service fees", like annual fee. Historically American Express and Capital One were of this type. In a modern world of free consumer cards, this type of banks becomes more and more rare, as the companies move to more sounds business models.

Servicing merchants

These are the guys you want to deal with. They derive most of their income from just servicing your cards. When you pay with your credit card, the merchant pays a fee. This fee is divided between two banks, the bank, which handles the merchant's account, and the bank which issued you the credit card. Most of their services for you are free.

More and more banks follow this business model, which proved itself viable and prudent. The clear leaders in this area are Bank One with their First USA cards, American Express with their Cashback and Optima cards, Discover, Chase Manhattan, and Citibank. Of course, that's not an authoritative list, just a personal opinion of this book's author. The important thing is that these are the banks you want to deal with. Not because they are listed here, but because they fit into what will be said below.

What to look for in a credit card?

- Grace period is a must. You should have at least three-four weeks grace period to pay your statement balance in full to avoid any interest charges.

- No annual fee. That's now an industry standard, and you are not in Europe, where credit card is a hard earned privilege. It must be free.

- Guarantees and protection against unauthorized charges. Best cards protect you both in store and online, and protect you 100%.

- Free online access. One of the advantages of a credit card is that though a credit card company gets a lot of private information on you and your spending habits, it actually shares this information with you! And, as you will see later in this book, if it does, that's well worth the trouble.

- Cashbacks. Good cards give you a cashback in some form. Examples include Chase's Shell Platinum MasterCard, American Express Cashback card, Discover, First USA eCard and Borders cards. Consider however, if cashback conditions are realistic for you. Some cards require you to spend a lot to get anything back. Cards without such conditions, like Shell or eCard, mentioned above, are much better in this sense. Notice, that annual cashback usually cannot exceed $200 or so. However, that's still money. They will not save you, but it's better to have them rather than not.

What does not matter in a credit card?

- Rate. You should not use credit card for the credit, remember? Hence you'll never get into the situation, where the rate is important.

- Cash advance conditions. In an emergency you can pay even a ridiculous price. Otherwise you don't want to use the credit card for cash advances anyway.

- Perks. You don't have time to remember and really use them.

- "Credit protection." That's insurance in a case you cannot pay your minimum balance fee. Everybody offers it, because it effectively makes your rate greater. There could be circumstances, when you may agree to that. In most cases, you don't want it.

What should you never accept in a credit card?

If a credit card offer contains anything listed below, just throw it away.

- Annual fee. See above.

- No grace period. See above.

- Your responsibility for unauthorized use. See above.

- No online access. See above.

Step 1: Identify your assets

What assets?

Generally, for our purposes, an asset is something that brings or can bring you money. Yes, it's that simple. What we want to do during this step is to identify all your potential assets and assess their current condition and value. For most of us the list of assets, that really bring money, is very simple:

Name of asset	Income per year
Salary	$XX,XXX.--

Notice, that because it's not exactly accounting, we put a bit different meaning in this word than a professional accountant would do. In accounting, asset is something you own, as opposed to liability, which is something you owe. You have a lot of personal items: the house, the cars, toilet paper in the bathroom. For accounting purposes, that's all "assets." For our purposes we talk only about something you have, which can bring you money. As a result it will also include the things usually kept out of the books, like job, ideas and skills.

Getting even deeper into accounting, we could find that all these are still assets. Your salary belongs to accounts receivables, and skills are intangible assets. But again, to use them as accountant, you should be an accountant, and most of us are not. Besides, we want something practical and working, even if it does not follow some high theory. So instead of using complicated accounting language, we will just call anything that brings us money an asset.

For such assets we need more information than just what they bring right now. We need to know what they potentially can bring, their current status, and how much effort is needed to change their status, so that they will start to bring money. The table will look like:

Name	Status	Effort	Potential income	Current income

How to find assets?

Now you need to brainstorm to find all or most of the assets, you have. Better do that together, but you can start it alone. Think of all potential ways to earn money. At this time, it does not matter how ridiculous they are, and you don't need to arrange them in any special order, just list everything, which will come to your head. Of course, don't list what you are certainly not going to do, or just cross it out immediately, so that it does not stand in a way.

Let consider an abstract example of a family of Dick and Jane with two children, partially paid-off house, and one salary. Here is how their list of assets could look like.

Name	Status	Effort	Potential income	Current income
Dick's salary as software developer	Active	-	-	$75,000.--/yr.
Jane's salary as software developer	No job now, good profession, but tough times to find a new job.	High	$55,000.--/yr	-
Jane's salary, non-professional	If no professional job can be found, Jane can take a low-income job	Medium	$10,000.--/yr?	-
Dick can write limericks and publish it in poetry magazines	None	Low	$100/yr? $10/yr?	-
House	Get a second mortgage?	Low	$25,000 one time?	-
Spend savings	One time thing, and we don't want to do that if possible	Low	$10,000 one time	
Jane can write a book on managing family finances	None	High	???	-
Sell old books from the basement on eBay	None	Low	$100 fixed?	-
Rent the first floor	None	Medium - High	$10,000/yr?	-
~~Rob a bank~~	~~Nah, we don't wanna do that.~~	~~High~~	~~$1,000,000?~~	-
…				
Total	Before taxes			$75000 or $6250 monthly

Notice, that classic accounting would say that cars, house, and some personal items are assets. But for our purposes, they are not, because they don't bring money. For us, asset is the first floor, which can be rented.

Dick and Jane also included two lines, which are not completely assets as we mean it, but can be used to get one time fixed amount of money. That's the old books, which can be sold, and paid off part of the house, for which they can get a second mortgage or home equity line.

This is a short sample list only. You will definitely have much longer list. If you have a computer, try to type it in. Even better, if you will use some spreadsheet software like Microsoft Excel. This will make your work with the list much easier. Look through the list and estimate feasibility of each option. Sort the list in order of most useful to least useful items. Look through it together again and discuss.

It's possible that at this point you will find some opportunity, and then you will immediately jump to the steps of increasing income. That will save you a lot of trouble, though generally some reasonable control over expenses is very useful, no matter how much money you make. So in any case, we recommend you to proceed to the next step, without passing some over.

Step 2: Identify your liabilities

What is a liability?

Just like with assets, liability is not exactly what is considered by this word in accounting. For our purposes liability is something that requires or will require expenses on your side. For example, formally and practically mortgage is your huge liability, but it's compensated by the value of the house. So just like with a house, we are not looking into the mortgage per se, but rather your mortgage payment.

Why not to call it just expenses? Because your expenses are just an amount of money, you have to come up with each month. Liability, on another hand, is the *reason* why you have to come up with this amount. Your income and expense analysis will just tell you how deep you are in a trouble. Assets and liabilities tell you how to get out of it.

How to identify your liabilities?

List of your active liabilities, the ones causing expenses now, is very easy to make. Take your bank statement, credit card statements, and pile of paid bills. Every check paid and every charge made to your credit card points out to some liability. Let's stress again, liability in the sense used by this book. For accounting a lot of stuff like "Food" or "My irresponsible behavior" are not liabilities, but for you and your family budget, they are. You don't need exact numbers at this time, you need just the names and very rough numbers.

Just like with assets, there are a number of things you should know about your liabilities. Here is a table:

Name	Status	Critical?	Future demand	Current expenses

Let consider again Dick and Jane's family as an example. Their first draft may look like:

Name	Status	Critical?	Future demand	Current monthly expenses
Mortgage (monthly payment)	Current, still 29 years to pay	Inevitable, even if we'll sell the house, we'll need to pay a rent.	-	$1700.--
Car payment	Current, still 3 years to pay	We need a car	-	$350.--
Living expenses:				
Utilities	Need more estimates	Yes	-	? $500 ?
Food	Need more estimates	Yes	-	? $600 ?
Dress	Need more estimates	Yes	-	? $100 ?
Family fun	Need more estimates	Yes	-	? $200 ?
Dick's hobby	Need more estimates	Dick wants it	-	? $200 ?
Jane's hobby	Need more estimates	Jane wants it	-	? $200 ?

Sport club	Mostly benefit from Dick's work	Yes	-	$70
Health	$100/yr after insurance	Yes	-	$10
Dentists	$600/yr after insurance	Maybe	-	$50
Car insurance		Yes, could it be less?	-	$90
Home insurance		Yes, could it be less?	-	$70
Taxes (income, social security, state, etc.)	$20000/yr	Yes		~$1700
Property tax	$3000/yr	Alas!	-	$250
Impulsive buys	Ouch...	No	-	$300
Celebrations	~$300 per birthday, ~$1200 Christmas	For kids, yes	-	~$200
Son's college	No idea, between $5k and $50K per year for 6 years	Yes	$30K-$300K, in 4 years	-
Daughter's college	No idea, between $5k and $50K per year for 6 years	Yes	$30K-$300K, in 6 years	-
Our retirement	$1000000. ?	Hopefully	In 20 years	
...				
Subtotal			Ouch!	$6590
Unexpected expenses	Add 10%			
Total	No, it could not be so much...			$7249 or ~$87K per year

Again, if you have a computer, try to use some spreadsheet software like Microsoft Excel (part of Microsoft Office). It will help you in a future, and nicely takes care of summing up subtotals as well as some intermediate results. It also will allow you to see easily both monthly and yearly view.

Your list is likely to have different numbers, but most categories will be the same. As you see a lot of digits are not clear, and very rough, but that's ok at this time. You will work on that later. What's important now is to get a systematic approach to what feeds on your budget and roughly how far off the target you are.

As you see, generally Dick and Jane need about $1000 monthly ($12000 per year) just to meet the ends, and that's before any savings. That's too bad, if you keep in mind need for the savings and future expenses. On another hand it looks like a manageable amount of money, which can be mostly covered, even with a low level job for Jane which is relatively easy to find. Or by renting the first floor to somebody.

You also see how long Dick and Jane can survive before the end of the road comes. With current spending rate and by using the savings, they can survive for almost a year without changes. Second mortgage will make them running for about a year and a half more. It's not two years, as it looks like, because it will add to liabilities and expenses.

Another thing, this table tells, is what are the biggest expenses, and what are the largest non-necessary expenses? It helps you to answer a question if there are some evident reserves, like stopping impulsive shopping or cutting birthday celebrations for adult members of the family.

Your numbers will be different. Look at them, what are they telling you?

- How much more you need monthly/yearly?

- How long you can survive with current status of the things?

- Is there something you can gain?

- Is there some liabilities, from which you can easily free yourself?

- What are your largest liabilities? What are your largest unnecessary liabilities?

Some readers may already have found the key to solving a puzzle and on the way to resolve their budget problems, but it's more likely that you have not. And even if you got some ideas already, don't hurry before you perform next two steps, which will allow you to answer the same questions with more precision.

Step 3: What's your income?

Now it's time to get from assets to actual income. For most of us the list will be very simple:

Name of asset	Income per year
Salary	$XX,XXX.--

It could be two salaries. Or you may have some other income. May be you occasionally do a contract work or publish paid articles in your professional area or something else. Whatever it is, put it here. Also if your company practices bonuses, visible from the budget point of view, put here what you expect or already got this year. What makes a visible amount is up to you to decide, but usually fifty bucks are not visible, while a thousand makes some difference.

Occasional buck-or-two does not have to go to this table. Similarly, don't list here income, which you could get, but not getting now. In contrast to assets, this is all about where exactly you are standing now. Then the table will look like:

Name of asset	Income per year
Salary	$XX,XXX.--
Total	$XX,XXX.--
Taxes (xx%)	-$YY,YYY.--
After tax income	$ZZ,ZZZ.--

The easiest way to find the number for taxes is to look at your federal and state tax returns for the last year. Beware that there is no single number anywhere. Your federal tax return lists in different places separately the total amount of federal income tax, you finally paid, and separately what you have paid to social security and Medicare. Add state income tax, if any, from the state tax return.

Generally taxes should be accounted in expenses, but getting them out immediately gets you straight to the bottom line, because these are the taxes which are anyway there. Yes, it nice that your employer carries such a burden on your behalf, but this money just never make it to your pocket, so it's the same as if it didn't exist for you. If you never did this exercise, which is doubtful, you will be surprised how much you pay to the state. Your federal tax return may have a notice of "effective rate" you are paying. And it often does not look bad, just 10-15%. But that's just federal income tax. When you add social security, Medicare, and state taxes, the actual rate may become almost shocking.

If you don't have your tax returns at hand, you can use just your latest pay stub for all these digits. Just don't forget to include your last federal and state tax rebates as additional lines right after the tax row.

Now let consider Dick and Jane's budget again as an example:

Name of asset	Income per month	Income per year
Salary	$6150	$73,800
Bonus	$100	$1,200
Total	$6250	$75,000
Taxes (26%)	~ -$1666	-$20,000
After tax income	~$4580	$55,000

Underlined numbers are the ones taken from documents. Other numbers are just calculated, except actual break between salary and bonus, which you are likely to remember. If you cannot, don't worry, it's ok to consider these two numbers together.

If Dick and Jane would use pay stubs the table would look like:

Name of asset	Income per month	Income per year
Salary	$6250	$75,000
Taxes (26%)	~ -$1830	-$21,960
After tax pay	~$4420	$53,040
Tax rebates	~$164	$1,960
After tax income	~$4580	$55,000

Getting exactly your income is tedious task, but it have to be done so that you know where exactly you are standing and what cash you have at hands. It's possible to live without such knowledge, but it's usually much more expensive.

Now it's time for you to write similar table. If you have not followed our advice, and don't use a computer, you can fill it right here:

Name of asset	Income per month	Income per year
First salary		
First bonus		
Second salary		
Second bonus		
Total		
Taxes (_____%)		
After tax income		

Step 4: What are your expenses

Just like with assets and income, we need to go from liabilities to actual expenses. You can start from the list of liabilities, making it more detailed and accurate and removing liabilities, which will lead to expenses in the future. That does not mean that they go away. But as long as we are not planning finances, but just trying to survive, it may be enough just to be aware of them. That's another reason of doing list of liabilities before going to expenses.

Making the list more detailed will include some work of getting the right numbers, instead of guessing. It also will make the list much longer, because smaller items will appear on it. For example, single line "Utilities" may become something like:

Item	Critical?	Expenses per month	Category subtotals
Electricity	Yes	~$40-100	
Gas	Yes	~$60-120	
Water	Yes	$20.--	
Sewer	Yes (big surprise)	$15.--	
Garbage removal	Yes	$25	
Phone (local)	Yes	$30.--	
Phone (long distance)	Yes, calling Jane's parents	$25.--	
Dick's cell phone	80%	$13.--	
Jane's cell phone	80%, kids use it to call home	$23.--	
Gasoline for cars	Yes	~$90	
Total Utilities			~$341-461

Notice that for expenses, columns "Status" and "Future demand" don't make any sense. But it's a good idea to separate each item expenses and subtotals by category of expenses in different columns. That will make the picture much more visible. Complete list for Dick and Jane would take too long, so we show here just one category. You will need to do the same for all categories.

Keep in mind, that you should include only periodical expenses. If some non-periodical expenses are large enough, you need to estimate how much you need for this kind of expenses per year and divide it by 12 for monthly number. And in most cases, "estimate" is just an importantly looking replacement for "your best guess."

So how do you find all this digits? Here are few tips.

Paper trail

Bills

The #1 source of information for you is bills. Some of them, like your mortgage, cable TV or Internet access, are very simple. They contain just a fixed monthly payment, which you just copy into appropriate cell of the table.

Some others have an amount, which varies from time to time. Such are bills for water, electricity, long distance calls, and, sometimes, cellular phone. For such bills you should try to estimate an average over the year. For example, if you electrical bill is $50 in summer and $150 in winter, then it is a safe bet to put $100-$120 as an estimate. It's better to err on the higher estimate, but try to avoid too high error anyway. Remember, you want the real picture, not over-optimistic one, and not a doomsday prophet declaration either.

Even better way to get an estimate is to have all your bills for a year summed up. Of course, it's often impossible or too complicated to be worth the trouble. But if you have these numbers handy, go for it. This gives you an exact number, and you need just add 5% for inflation to have pretty good estimate for the next year.

Of course, keep in mind that inflation numbers vary with a time. The official government inflation numbers may be not so useful, because the prices grow differently in different categories. For example, for last few years gasoline prices surged from $1.10 per gallon to about $1.80 per gallon (actual prices vary by state), which is about 40% raise. On another hand the cheapest bread in your neighborhood store is likely to be still $1, just like it was 5-6 years ago.

Use duplicate checks

Duplicate checks are a bit more expensive than single ones, but they give you a handy record on what, when and to whom you paid. With more and more banks trying to dispose used checks instead of returning them to you, duplicate checks become even more useful. And if you don't download transactions from the bank web site to your accounting software, duplicate checks become sometimes invaluable.

Except keeping a record, duplicate checks allow you to see immediately what you have paid recently. Are you subscribed to any magazine? How many invoices for subscription renewal are you getting? It's likely that dozens, with some of invoices coming after you actually paid. And if you are like the rest of us, I mean, not a super-being, you don't remember that. Did you ever paid on separate invoices for 2-3 years ahead? Some of us do. Duplicate checks help to prevent such confusion.

Used checks

Most banks prefer not to return your checks with your statement. But if yours does, that's another source of information, you can use.

Getting back your used checks from the bank has certain cons and pros, which are discussed later. But as a paper trail and evidence of payment they are the good thing.

Use a computer

Many families have a computer at home. If you have one, use it! If you don't, just accounting may be not worth buying it. Although I know the family, keeping an old computer in the kitchen specially for accounting, recipes, and similar small stuff. There is a number of ways, computer can help you to manage your finances, and here are just few of them.

Use accounting software

Most popular ones are Quicken and Microsoft Money. For a long time Quicken was the unchallenged champion, but lately more and more favorable reviews go to MS Money, and so they are probably on par with each other right now. Of course, using 100% of either program requires a Ph.D. in Corporate Logic, which was used to design it. And wasting your time on that is not necessary to your advantage. Just leave obscure features to obscure people and stick with 20% of features used by 80% of users. You still will get keeping records substantially simpler.

If you have used such a program for a year, you already have all necessary data right at your fingertips. Getting the total for a year comes almost with a snap of fingers. Just use reports, if you can figure out which buttons to press. Just sorting all transaction by the name on the check with a little help of old fashioned calculator does the same thing. Anyway, figuring out how much you paid for particular service is not a problem anymore.

One of standard reports in both programs is income and expense, and it is especially useful. You instantly see your monthly income and expenses for any period of time, when you have been keeping records. You also see the difference, and where most of your money go. On another hand, it does not free you from doing these manual tables of your income and expense. Automatic reports are great, but they have their own problems. For example, fluctuation of a payment day between 30th and 1st of the next month will make this report look like you have missed some income in one month and gained much more in another. Depending on how you keep you records, this report may be incomplete and even misleading. For example, getting a bunch of cash from your account and saving it in a pillow for emergency may be considered by such program as an expense. At the same time keeping an account for allowances, you give your kids, may make these money pile up and look like you still have them, even after they were actually spent on ice cream and bicycles.

Download transactions

One bank burglar was asked, why he is robbing the banks? "Because that's where the money is," was the answer. This little wisdom can be applied to non-material objects as well. Instead of tormenting yourself with entering all checks, store receipts, and bank statements into your computer, just ask yourself, where all this information is? Right, it's all in the bank.

Another advantage of Information Age is ability to download all you transactions from your bank web site directly into your accounting software. This simplifies getting everything recorded and helps to ensure that you will have enough data for decision making.

Even if you don't use accounting software, you still can view all the latest transactions. That's less helpful, but it's still very convenient.

Use the right bank

As already mentioned, your banks may be very helpful in getting everything right. That's why it is so important to choose the right one. There are basically two important criteria when making such a decision: how much the bank gets from you, and what you get from the bank. We already discussed what should be the credit card, now let see what do you want from checking, saving, and money market accounts.

Free checking

No service fee is a must. You can accept service fee, if balance goes below certain amount, if you are sure that's the amount you are going to have at all times. Because a single account is unlikely to reflect your overall assets, but just a small part of them, it's wise to see for relatively low limits. For example, service fee for balances below $100 is probably ok. After all, why would you need an account for less than $100? And service fee for balances below $5000 is definitely not ok. If you have few extra grands, you definitely can use them better than to satisfy your banker's corporate logic, which is best described with Duffy's "Mine, mine, mine!"

Returned checks

Most banks today are trying to sell "safekeeping" feature. That means that you don't see your used and paid checks, but can get a copy of them. The bank is interested in this, because getting the actual paper checks back to you is a substantial effort. It's substantially more cheap to scan them at the source and destroy, instead of actually sending it to your processing center and putting into a folder, not to mention getting it into your envelope. Of course, a lot of operations here are automatic, but still it's cheaper.

This is true, that returned checks are usually a waste of space and theoretically represent a security risk. So from this point of view, you may want to agree with your bank on that. Unless, of course, it's insolent enough to ask for a fee for this "service."

However, in a case of a dispute, with returned checks you have a proof of payment. And this proof is at hands, whenever you need it. It's true, that most banks allow you to order a copy or get one from Internet, but consider just two factors before making your mind:

1. Banks don't keep your checks forever. Online access is even more limited in time. What if you need a proof of payment in a year or two?

2. Getting a check from your folder is much faster and simpler than getting one from Internet or by ordering it by phone. Remember, most disputes don't look serious enough at the beginning, but they

are much easier to fix at the beginning. Easy access to returned checks may save you a substantial loss of time and peace of mind later. It did for me a couple of times.

Of course, these reasons are not absolute, and you may decide that it's not important for you. So just make up your mind.

Free ATM card

Free ATM is important, but tough to get. Anyway, try to minimize potential ATM fees, because that's what you are going to use.

Once I had an "absolutely free checking," which still charged for getting cash from ATM. I just did not read the fine print carefully. Guess what, the first month of this "absolutely free checking" cost me few times more than if it would have a service fee of $5-10, but really free ATM.

You most definitely know all this, but let clarify and bring a system to various ATM fees. When you make an ATM transaction, there are four participants in the process: you, bank, servicing an ATM machine, ATM network like Cirrus or Star, and your bank. You don't charge yourself. Expenses of ATM network are always on the bank. The question is if they pass them on you or not, but directly this is the bank's problem. Now we left with two participants, who can charge you: bank owning the ATM machine, and your bank.

Bank, which owns ATM machine, may charge you or your bank. In the first case, you just see the prompt and can decide, if you need cash so badly as to pay that $1.00-$1.50, or not. Your bank may offer up to 2 to 5 rebates per month for such charges, and that's a nice thing to have. Other than that, that's pretty much all you can do about such charges.

Your bank has much more opportunities to charge you. First, it can establish a monthly or annual fee for an ATM card. Just don't go for it. Even if it's small, it's a clear lack of a good faith in relations, and such bank eventually will be a problem.

There are, of course, exceptions. Sometimes bank offers alternatively ATM card and something like "VISA Check Card." Cut the crap about "VISA check card is accepted everywhere, where VISA credit cards are accepted." It does not. Just consider it another form of ATM card. If one of them has a fee, and another is free, go for the free one. As ATM cards they work exactly the same way. The fee in this case is just a way for your bank to ask you to choose one over another.

Second fee associated with an ATM card is per use fee. Basically your bank may want something around $1.00 each time you use your ATM card to get cash. That's a definite no-no. Don't go for it. With such charges you better off with a service fee. Besides, if your bank is so stupid or relies on so stupid customers, do you know what it will invent the next time to get into your pockets?

Third type of fee is a kind of the second one. Your bank may charge you only if you are using "foreign" ATM machine. "Foreign" does not mean Swedish or British, it means "machine of another bank." You may think that your bank is trying to compensate the same fee, you are asked to pay by some cash machine, but you will be wrong. The same transaction may end up with a $1.50 fee from cash machine bank, and another $1.50 from your bank for using a "foreign ATM," leaving you with $3.00 fee. Before agreeing to such terms, check if you bank has ATM machines everywhere, where you need them. Close to your work, close to your home, close to the places, where you usually shop. If so, it may still be acceptable.

Notice that these are just generic rules, you need to get a clear answer from your bank about fees, because the fantasy is not limited by such straightforward schemas. For example, one of the dominant banks on the West coast had a policy, that just getting cash was a subject to fee, while getting "express cash" was not. So by inadvertently pressing a wrong button you were paying the bank just for that: for pressing a wrong button! Everything else was, as you can guess, exactly the same. So, *emptor caveat*, be careful!

Online access

If you have Internet access, online access to your account is important. It gives you ability to check what's going on very quickly, without trying to explain what you want to a bank clerk over the phone. It allows you to download transactions into your accounting software, and save the trouble of typing everything in.

Online access must be free. Just a few years ago some banks were trying to make money on it, putting some ridiculous restrictions, like "four downloads per month is free." That does not work. Unless your computer will have automatic workflow engine and support automatic downloads 4 times a month, you will end up with more, and anyway, you still may want a spontaneous access to your account information.

There are a lot of variations on how online access is done. And often it's not done in the best way. For example, the same bank, which was charging its own customers for pressing a wrong button on ATM machine, requires to use Social Security Number as online logon ID. Many people are rightfully uncomfortable about that, but, hey, that's less load on corporate servers, right? And who can count the people who don't use online services of this bank or don't bank with them because of that. So, choose wisely.

Most popular problems with online access are:

- Attempt to make money on online access.

- Substantial downtime.

- Non-integrated visual (from browser) and automatic (from accounting software) access, with different logon IDs.

- Inflexible User ID and password policies, like using SSN as ID.

It's a great temptation to recommend asking your friends about their experience with some bank before opening an account there. But the truth is that friends advice does not work very well. The fact that she or he is your friend does not mean that you want the same things from the bank, even less from the bank's online access. You may want automatic download, and your friend may have fun just entering her SSN in the browser. People differ, even friends.

The best online services, I ever encountered were Bank One, its affiliate First USA (credit cards), and American Express. Visual and automatic service are integrated, online access is free, almost always up, and download happen smoothly right out you accounting software. There could be other banks with as impressive services, but I am not aware of them.

Step 5: What's the deficit?

This is a very easy and simple step, but it will define everything, you will do later in the process. You have your income, you have your expenses, now get the difference. Account for taxes only on one side. That is, if you taking your gross income subtract expenses including all taxes, and if you took your income after the taxes, subtract expenses without the taxes already accounted for. The difference is how much after tax money you need.

"After-tax" mean unpleasant reminder, that to cover it with new income, you need earn not just this amount, but also the taxes, which you will have to pay additionally for greater income. If you will do that by cutting expenses, you are ok, because expenses you pay with after-tax money anyway.

Now make the first memo to yourself:

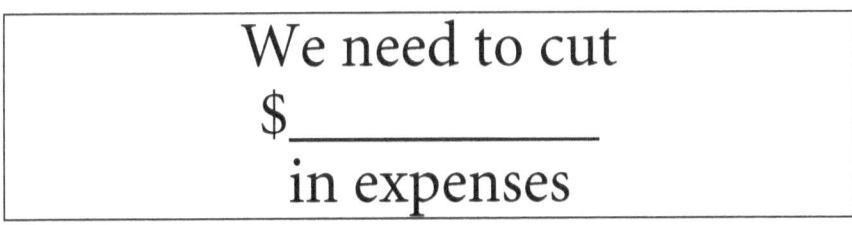

Let suppose you cannot cut so much expenses. We don't know yet, may be you could, but what if? Then you need extra income, right?

How to estimate taxes to get the amount of additional income, you need? The first thing you need is to know your taxable income. Taxable income is basically your income minus various deductions and "exceptions." If you are in a tough situation already for some time, and your income and expenses have not changed much since last year, your best bet would be to look at the number on your last year tax report.

However, the chances are that you have changes. In this case try the simplified method below. It's not something, you can really use for your taxes, and it's not something, which will stay forever. These estimates are based on 2001 taxes. In 10 years all numbers most certainly will be substantially different. Even in 2002 they are going to be somewhat different. Also this method is based on the rate for families, if you are single or filing as a head of household, you will need to adjust the numbers. But still you will get pretty good idea about what to expect.

So here is the method. We will illustrate it on the Dick and Jane's example:

1	Write down your gross income	$75,000
2	Sum up deductions accounted for calculation of Adjustable Gross Income, like IRA contributions within limits, interest on student loans, moving expenses, if you qualify, half of self-employment tax, if you have any.	$0
3	Estimate your standard or itemized deductions. If you used itemized deductions last year, it's likely to be a good estimate this year too. If you used a standard deductions, for 2001 it was $7600 for families (married, filed jointly)	$17,000
4	Multiply $2900 to number of children+2 (for married)	$11,600
5	Subtract 2, 3, and 4 from 1, here is a rough estimate of your taxable income.	$46,400

As you see, line 2 for Dick and Jane is 0, because they don't have anything like mentioned in the list. Line 3 is the itemized deduction taken from the last year return and rounded down to be on the safe side. Line 4 is just $2900 multiplied by 4 (2 for Dick and Jane, and 2 for the kids.)

Now make similar computations for yourself:

1	Write down your gross income	$_____
2	Sum up deductions accounted for calculation of Adjustable Gross Income, like IRA contributions within limits, interest on student loans, moving expenses, if you qualify, half of self-employment tax, if you have any.	$_____
3	Estimate your standard or itemized deductions. If you used itemized deductions last year, it's likely to be a good estimate this year too. If you used a standard deductions, for 2001 it was $7600 for families (married, filed jointly)	$_____
4	Multiply $2900 to number of children+2 (for married)	$_____
5	Subtract 2, 3, and 4 from 1, here is a rough estimate of your taxable income.	$_____

Now when you have an estimate of you taxable income, you can try to figure out how much different governments will want from your extra income. Let start from the federal one. Below are the table for 2001. Years 2002 and later will have different tax tables, so you can get a better estimate by going to http://www.irs.gov and getting instruction for the latest year available. If it's complicated, use 2001 tables in the end of this chapter. After all it's unlikely that taxes will be substantially decreased, and it unlikely that they will be substantially increased. Of course, there is George Bush's tax cut, but it's better to err on the negative side.

As you see, Dick and Jane got lucky, if low income can be classified as "luck", and most of their income was taxed at the lowest 15% rate. Only $1200 was taxed at 27.5% and they have a plenty of space in this tax bracket. Namely, every extra $1000, Dick and Jane will earn, will be taxed at 27.5% up to the moment, when their taxable income will become $109,500. In other words, Dick and Jane can earn roughly extra $62 thousands without leaving their tax bracket.

On the negative side 27.5% is a lot of money. That's $275 from each $1000! This way from each extra $1000 Dick and Jane are getting only $725. Ouch! And that's just a beginning, because we did not counted state, social security, and Medicare yet.

For state tax the simplest strategy would be to take the numbers of a state tax and federal tax for the last year, and divide one to another. Then multiply this number to your estimate of the federal tax per $1000. For example, if Dick and Jane last year federal tax was $6700, and state tax was $1107, then the ratio is 1107/6700 = 16.5% and estimate of the state tax per thousand will be around $275*16.5% or about $45.

This method has one serious danger, which you may already noticed. What if compared to last year, you have moved to a new tax bracket? For Dick and Jane that meant moving from 15% to 27.5% on federal taxes. Can the state tax jump similarly? Of course, it can. So, your best tactic would be to get your state income tax instructions for the latest year available, and find the actual table there.

Similarly to estimates of the state tax, you can try to estimate social security and Medicare deductions from your paycheck. Look at the last year W-2 forms. Notice, that your tax return actually does not contain these numbers. The actual result, you will get, depends on your particular numbers. But don't be surprised, if they'll make around 30% of your federal tax.

Again this method has underwater rocks. For example, when you get to some amount on your social security tax, it's stopped from being deducted until the end of the year. This amount depends on the year. In 2001 it was $4984.80. However to get to this amount, you need to have a relatively high personal salary. In 2001 it had to be more than $80,400 per year to hit this limit. Notice, that's not your combined salary, but individual salary. Each of you will pay up to this limit.

Another place where federal tax, social security, and Medicare numbers get together, is your paycheck. But it's not a good source of estimate, because the federal tax withholdings are not yet adjusted to what actually will be in your tax return.

Now getting back to Dick and Jane. Let assume their estimate for social security and Medicare is 30%, that's about $82. So for every $1000 different governments will get about $275+$45+$82, or about $402, leaving them with just $598. Now again is a time for a worksheet:

1	For every	$1000
2	Federal tax is	$275
3	State tax is about	$45
4	Social security and Medicare taxes are	$82
5	So total taxes are (add up lines 2, 3, and 4)	$402
6	And we are getting (subtract line 5 from line 1)	$598
7	or (divide line 6 on line 1)	0.598 or 59.8%
8	So to get $1000, we have to earn (divide $1000 by line 7)	$1672
9	So the proportion of earned vs. actual income is (divide line 8 by 1000)	$1.672
10	Our annual deficit is (the number from the beginning of this chapter)	$12,000
11	So we need to earn (multiply lines 9 and 10)	$20,064

That hurts, right? Now make the calculations for yourself:

1	For every	$1000
2	Federal tax is	$
3	State tax is about	$
4	Social security and Medicare taxes are	$
5	So total taxes are (add up lines 2, 3, and 4)	$
6	And we are getting (subtract line 5 from line 1)	$
7	or (divide line 6 on line 1)	
8	So to get $1000, we have to earn (divide $1000 by line 7)	$
9	So the proportion of earned vs. actual income is (divide line 8 by 1000)	$
10	Our annual deficit is (the number from the beginning of this chapter)	$
11	So we need to earn (multiply lines 9 and 10)	$

Now make a memo for yourself:

Or we need to earn
$ _____
more.

Now you are equipped with two numbers of your budget deficit. One is how much expenses you need to cut. Another one, is how much your need to earn, if you cannot cut expenses. In real life it could be a bit of both, so keep the ratio from line 9 above between expenses and earnings, necessary to cover the expenses.

Federal tax estimates based on 2001 data

If you are married...*

For every $1000 between		you are paying	
From	To	Amount	Percentage
$0	$45,200.00	$150	15%
$45,200.00	$109,250.00	$275	27.5%
$109,250.00	$166,500.00	$305	30.5%
$166,500.00	$297,350.00	$355	35.5%
$297,350.00	and up	$391	39.1%

* Based of 2001 federal income tax. Should not be used for official tax purposes. For other years numbers will be different.

If you are married, but filing separately...*

The picture will be basically the same, but scaled twice, so that each of you can earn his or her own half of what is allowed in each tax bracket. Just for reference, here is the table. Keep in mind, when you add numbers from your tax return to your spouse tax return, the digits will be the same as above.

For every $1000 between		you are paying	
From	To	Amount	Percentage
$0	$22,600.00	$150	15%
$22,600.00	$54,625.00	$275	27.5%
$54,625.00	$83,250.00	$305	30.5%
$83,250.00	$148,672.00	$355	35.5%
$148,672.00	and up	$391	39.1%

* Based of 2001 federal income tax. Should not be used for official tax purposes. For other years numbers will be different.

If you are filing as a head of household...*

For every $1000 between		you are paying	
From	To	Amount	Percentage
$0	$36,250.00	$150	15%
$36,250.00	$93,650.00	$275	27.5%
$93,650.00	$$151,650.00	$305	30.5%
$151,650.00	$297,350.00	$355	35.5%
$297,350.00	and up	$391	39.1%

* Based of 2001 federal income tax. Should not be used for official tax purposes. For other years numbers will be different.

And in a case, you are single...*

For every $1000 between		you are paying	
From	To	Amount	Percentage
$0	$27,050.00	$150	15%
$27,050.00	$65,550.00	$275	27.5%
$65,550.00	$136,750.00	$305	30.5%
$136,750.00	$297,350.00	$355	35.5%
$297,350.00	and up	$391	39.1%

* Based of 2001 federal income tax. Should not be used for official tax purposes. For other years numbers will be different.

Step 6: Handle your necessary predictable expenses first

Determine your necessary expenses

This step will not decrease your expenses and will not bring you extra income. However it will help to ensure, that whatever you do, you will have your necessary expenses covered.

First consider your expenses data, you prepared above. Select from there all really necessary expenses. That is absolutely necessary expenses, which are letting you to continue running. Basically, this is housing and main utilities. Dick and Jane's list will look like:

Item	Expenses per month
Mortgage payment	$1700
with escrow (property tax + insurance)	$275
Electricity	~$40-100
Gas	~$60-120
Water	$20.--
Phone (local)	$30.--
Sewer	$15.--
Garbage removal	$25
Gasoline for cars	~$90
Car insurance	$90
Total	$2345-2465
Monthly after-tax income	$4580
Free after necessary expenses	$2235-2115

Notice that we immediately calculate the money left after these necessary expenses. That's the amount you can use for all other needs, not included into this list.

Among ones is the food. Is food really not necessary? Of course not. However the nature of food expenses is such that they have to be handled separately. See it below in following steps.

We have not listed long distance phone service. Though important, usually it is not absolutely necessary. To keep you local phone service detached from long distance service, use phone cards. In summer 2002, when this book was written, at Costco there were MCI calling cards with a rate of about 3.5 cents a minute without any surcharges. It's tough to beat this, you get control over long distance calls, and you'll never get your phone disconnected because of long distance bill.

Notice that keeping services separately from each other is generally a very powerful tool. Imagine that you are using some Internet access provider. Together with Internet access, you've got email address. Would it be wise to use one? Imagine that your provider got you very disappointed, which is not a big surprise in modern days. Switching Internet access provider is easy, switching email address is not. All your friends know this address, and getting them on a new one is a lot of trouble. Companies love when you select "bundled deals." They tell you that this is a great "win-win" offers. In rare cases it is. However most of the times, it is not. The company definitely wins, that's why the love bundling services. You need to think at least twice before buying on that. And don't bundle really necessary things with a cool stuff. You may be hooked up on it even when it will not be cool for you anymore.

Now let's get back to your necessary expenses. Your list is likely to be different. For example, you may have car loan payment, and you definitely need a car to get to and from work. Or you may live in a metropolitan area and use the local transit. Then car, gasoline, and car insurance are not a must for you, but expenses for the bus are. Similarly, you may have rent instead of mortgage, home insurance and property tax.

In essence, only you can decide, what is absolutely necessary. Just be realistic and honest with yourself, for most of us restaurants and manicure is not absolutely necessary, and having a place to live is. Now do so. We would recommend to use the same spreadsheet, if you use computer, but in a case you did not, here is the table to fill:

Item	Expenses per month
Housing (mortgage + escrow or rent)	
Electricity	
Gas	
Water	
Phone (local)	
Sewer or septic tank service	
Garbage removal	
Gasoline for cars	
Car insurance	
Other transportation	
Total	
Monthly after-tax income	
Free after necessary expenses	

Look at what you've got. Do you have enough money after these necessary expenses? You don't need to come up with exact answer yet, but it's worth making a guess.

If you have none, something is terribly wrong. In most cases, unless you can get a much cheaper housing, you cannot survive on your income. Keep in mind, that you still need money for food, dress, medical and dental expenses, household needs like toothpaste, soap, shampoo, detergent, little repairs around the house. So if you see nothing left after the expenses listed above, skip directly to the steps on increasing your income. You still may have to cut some expenses, but it will not really help without extra income.

Separate main account

Now isolate these expenses from everything else. Just get a separate checking account, and put there every month the amount, you just calculated. Never use this account for anything, but paying these expenses. If you mistakenly estimated that expenses too high and money start to pile up on this account, you can move extra to the generic one. However keep in mind, that some of your expenses have seasonal fluctuations. Maybe the money pile up to pay for those winter electric and gas bills?

Technically, if you can, use direct deposit. Make this fixed amount go directly to this special account, and the rest of your salary to a generic account.

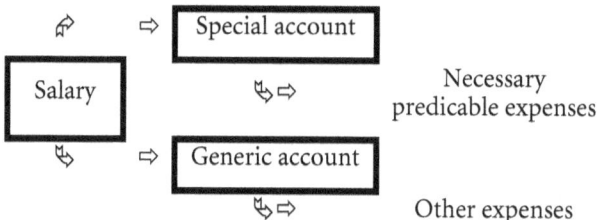

If your employer cannot send your salary to two accounts, send it all to this special account. And every time, you've got salary, move extra amount to a generic account. If both accounts are in the same bank, you may be able to setup automatic transfer for free.

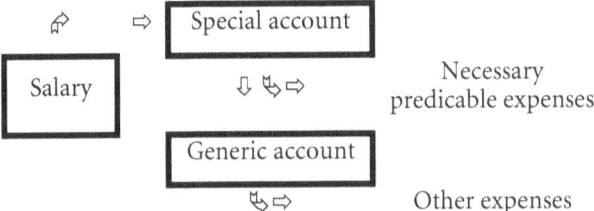

Don't move money other way around:

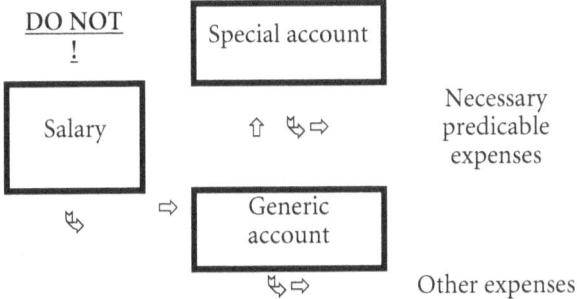

The reason is simple: if your generic account gets overdrafted, you may miss amount necessary to pay your critical expenses.

Can you still decrease some of these expenses?

Yes, by all means. If you can decrease some of these expenses, it is a very good idea to do so. For example, if you have a mortgage, and interest rates are favorable, by refinancing you can cut up to few hundreds from your monthly bill. Of course, the actual amount depends on your individual numbers, and you probably already did so in 2002, when mortgage rates were record low. So even if rates will fall further, which is unlikely, the effect probably will not be worth the trouble. But anyway, check for the possibility.

You can still work on other expenses. Maybe you often leave a lot of electric devices on, even when you don't need them. Or you could have kept the temperature at home like in sauna. Or may be you just cannot get all your garbage into a standard can, so that you are charged extra. If something like that happens, it may be a good time to change some of your habits. Just don't expect a lot out of it.

A generic rule is simple. Look at the big expenses. Try to do something about them. Look at other expenses. Try to do something reasonable about them. "Reasonable" means that you have the time and resources to go further, and not be stuck in this step.

A lot of people will tell you, that finances is the area, where it's worth to sweat on a small stuff. And they will be right. Just start from the big stuff first, and you will have a lot of it further in this book. You'll enjoy sweating on the small stuff later, if thinking big will prove to be insufficient.

Step 7: Finding and fighting nuisance expenses

Something, we don't even talk about

Gambling, sex outside of marriage, drugs…Whether you check with Torah, Bible, Koran, modern western ethical views, or laws of King Hammurapi (XVIII BC) all these things are sins. Even more they are financial sins committed against your family budget. Not surprisingly, this happens more often either in poor families, who have nothing to lose, or very wealthy ones, who can afford that. Middle class normally just cannot afford that.

A little clarification may be required. When we say "gambling", we don't mean subscribing through Publisher Clearing House. When we say "sex outside of marriage", we don't mean single people. When we say "drugs", we don't talk about antibiotic medicine prescribed by your doctor. Though we have opinion of all of this, that's not something that normally ruins people financially. And you should have pretty good idea now, what we are really talking about.

So if anything of this is part of your life, go to Step–1, and read it again. It says that any family member may become an insurmountable obstacle for getting the whole family out of trouble. If you are involved into anything like that, you are that member. You are the one, who gets the family into a trouble.

Fast food, restaurants, snacks

It's a surprising contrast. We are considered the nation, which in the eyes of the whole world looks like crazy about healthy style of life. At the same time we consume most of the fast food in the world. Hotdogs, pizzas, various burgers, and fries make a multi-billion industry today. Not to mention that this is not a healthy food, it's also bad for your pockets. Why? It's just a few bucks! Let see…

Of course, there is no much harm in an occasional Big Mac. Even though it's still few bucks, which could have a better use for both health and family. The actual problem happens not at the time, when you order and eat some fast food. It happens when you stop cooking for the family and start to depend on outside meals regularly.

Now let's do some math. Average meal at McDonald (cheeseburger, fries, soda) is about $5 per person. Family of 4 can get something for $15-17. $15 per day is about $450 per month, or $5,475 per year of after-tax money. And that is just dinners. You still need breakfast, lunch, some fruits and vegetables. Does it sounds like just a few bucks now? But that's just a beginning. Now let look into the problem deeper.

When fast food took you out of family cooking business, you depend on outside meals. And dining every day of your life in some fast food chain will make you suffer. Even if that are such great ones like McDonald or Burger King. You will need to go to something better, remember, you are not cooking for your family! And so $15 quickly becomes $40-50 and more. Of course, it's just occasional break in routine at the beginning, but the more you hate your usual fast food chain, the more often you go for such a break. Is it clear, what it does to your pockets?

If it's still does not sound convincing enough, I can add that uncomfortably high number of Americans have this problem. One my friend, who is a real estate agent, once had an interesting client to whom she was helping to buy a house. He was an engineer employed at Boeing, who worked there for about 20 years. He and his wife had no savings at all to use as a down payment. Basically everything they earned, they were immediately spending. He was not alcoholic, he did not gamble, he had a stable and well paid job, and still they had no savings at all. When they were asked how it happened, he answered, "You know, when I am getting from work we have to go somewhere to eat, and that's pretty expensive." Of course it could not be the only reason, but it was one of the reasons, why for 20 years they were not able to put aside even a small amount of money.

So how can you get of the hook? That depends on the reasons, why you got there in the first place. Here are some usual reasons.

"My mom never taught me…"

Well, she should had, but putting this aside, what do you do now? Amazingly, a lot of people just don't know how to make a meal. The reason is usually that nobody ever taught them how to do that. Daughters are not taught cooking because it's sexist, and boys are not taught that because they are boys. By the way, that usually happens in the same families, and nobody notices a logical contradiction here. That's not to mention that both reasons are plain false. Two centuries ago hunter, cowboy, or soldier had to know how to cook just to survive.

Putting ridiculous excuses aside, the main reason is that parents are too lazy or too indecisive to teach children to cook. And school just does not cover this subject. As a result, some people are just scared of the idea to make something on their own.

So what do you do, if this is your case? Try to start from something simple and fast. There are a lot of semi-prepared products, which require almost no time or effort to make.

For example, take two cans of Campbell Chunky soup (two servings per can), which is basically a main dish. Pour their content into a bowl, and heat in a microwave for 4-5 minutes. Add a slice of bread and glass of soda. You are done. The dinner for four is served. All your effort is opening two cans, 5 minutes at microwave, and throwing bowl and plates into the dishwasher. Or you can wash the plates immediately the old way, it will take less than a minute. Does it sounds hard to you?

Money-wise such dinner is also good. Let calculate:

Two cans of Campbell Chunky ($2.29 each) $4.58

Four slices of bread $0.10

A two-liter bottle of Coke on sale $1.00

Total: $5.68

Dinner for four in six minutes for six dollars! Compare to fast food $15 or regular restaurant $50. "Prosecution has nothing to add."

If you are just lazy or cannot decide, who should cook

If the husband is a president of "Men don't cook" club, and the wife is a proud leader of "Don't feed those sexist bastards" society, you are in a trouble anyway. Otherwise, get real. All this crap about men not cooking or women as slaves of a kitchen can wait until you will resolve more important family problems like money and budget. And anyway, whether you really believe it or not, that's just an excuse to avoid cooking. And there is only one true reason for that: you personally just don't want cooking. That's it.

That's true, that if you don't know how to cook, it may become a complex task at first. To resolve this problem, see above.

That's also true, that when you come after work, it's nice to get some rest, instead of doing some work in the kitchen. But again, look above. There is a lot of ways to make it simple.

And that's true, that working people just don't have much time. However, if the reason, why you have money problems, is that you live on one salary instead of two, one of you definitely got a lot of time. Just be nice to the other one and make your part.

If your life is so routine, that you just want to get out

Every day? Every meal? Something should be terribly wrong, with what you are doing beside the meals. Is your life really so boring that sterile walls of a fast food restaurant bring a life in it? Oh, man, money or not, you really should do something about that!

Did you ever try to read? Well, that's what you are doing right now, but I mean not to learn something, but just to have a good time? Some people enjoy going to concerts, theaters, and art galleries. Well, sure, we are not in Europe, and here a lot of people are not interested "in this crap", and frankly, often it is a crap. What about great outdoors? A weekend in a forest, stories around campfire, and sleeping in tents and sleeping bags could be a lot of fun.

No? Fine. Men can try to build something with their own hands. Say, that small table for newspapers, you wanted for so long. Women can try cooking, and I don't mean two cans of Campbell soup, but *real* cooking. Men, who know how to cook, enjoy this a lot as well.

If you have no kids

Do you have kids? If your life is so boring, it's likely that you don't. And if you don't, you should. If you can, don't cut the corners with an adoption. Get a child the hard way, the old-fashioned one. It has a lot of benefits to be a biological parent of your own child. And when you will get a child, your life will never be boring again.

Let me also talk to my readers, who belong to my own sex for a moment. Men, please, be gentlemen, and skip three paragraphs below.

So, girls, here is a good news for you, if you did not heard it yet. Some medical schools believe that pregnancy takes about 5 years off your biological clock. It happens because some cells of your child get into your bloodstream, carried all over your body, and settle down there, making your whole body younger.

That's exactly what they are doing in those million-dollar rejuvenation treatments for Hollywood stars, billionaires, and third world dictators, but with a few advantages. It costs you much less, it does not involve morally dubious materials, and the cells much better match your own DNA. Hey, half of this DNA is yours anyway! And another half belongs to your husband, which should feel good too.

Some believe the Nature rewards women this way for creating a new life. Some believe it's a God's idea. But both ways, it's great to be younger.

Ok, gentlemen! You are welcome back. We are coming to the topic, which will interest you a lot.

Do you love each other? I mean how much and how often?

Sad, but true. Five minute sex once a week is widespread in a national epidemic proportions. No need to admit that loudly, just think, does it sounds like your family life? If yes, no wonder, your life is so boring.

And that happens while tête-à-tête evening with candles at your own home may be worth a hundred dinners in restaurants. Some readers may say that I, probably, never was in expensive high-class restaurants with menus $200 per person. Yes, this is true, I was not. But let me ask you, did you ever have an intimate evening with your spouse, which is worth a hundred dinners in such restaurants? If it's not late, you still should try. And if you had, you know that for yourself.

Anyway, it's all boils down to a simple fact, that you can be the greatest hobby of each other. And boredom will become something, that you will have difficulty to understand, not to say experience.

If you hate each other...

There is another case, when people are forced to eat outside. That's the case when you hate each other so that everything you cook for each other is not consumable. That's known to happen. I don't even talk about scientifically unproven, but widely believed difference between food prepared with love, and the food prepared with hate. It's much simpler. When people cook for somebody they hate, they have to be very good professionals to avoid screwing up.

If this is the case, too bad. Go to "Step minus 1" and read it again. You have to do something about that, because among other, more important, but more subtle reasons, you just simply cannot afford hate.

Alcohol, smoking?

Alcohol and tobacco are the legal drugs. Yes, they are legal. But they are still addictive, and they hurt. Drinker accustomed to a 6-pack of $8 per pack beer per day spends $240 per month and $2920 per year. Smoker, who uses a pack per day of $40 per 10-pack cartoon of cigarettes, spends about $1460 per year. In both cases that is the money you could use better.

Alcohol also very negatively affects you ability to do your job, and does a number of other bad things to you. So you are not just spending good deal of money, you also potentially compromising your sources of income.

There is no sense to carry out anti-alcohol or anti-tobacco education in this book, because everybody knows everything about that. So if somebody continues, education hardly can help. Still, if you don't, stay away. If you do, but reasonably, keep it low and get it lower, if you can. Otherwise, the thought about family budget may actually help you to deal with these habits. It's hard to say, which end of the deal will be more beneficial to you.

Step 8: Are there expenses you can easily cut?

Look again at the tables of your liabilities and expenses. Start from liabilities. Is there something, which should not be there, when you have financial troubles? Do you really need everything on the list? We are trying to give you some hints below, but only you can decide what is really necessary, and what is not.

If you will look at Dick and Jane's example, there is no much on their list. Of cause, there is uncontrollable shopping. We will deal with it on the next step. There is a sport club and hobbies. However, the sport club is very important for the health, and health is something necessary both financially and generally. Hobbies are less critical, and it may be worth to slow down on them. However, something beside work is necessary for mental health, and unless you will find some alternative and less expensive hobby, you need something. However, it's possible to compensate for absence of such items. See below for more hints on the subject.

Suppose you had to walk through the list and found nothing or almost nothing to cut. "Almost nothing" means "insufficient to cover deficit." What do you do? You go to the expense list.

With expense list start first form large items. First filter anything more than $500. Can you do anything about anything in such list? It's very likely, that you cannot. But if there is something odd, something not necessary, that's definitely something to cut. Just two such items would get Dick and Jane out of trouble. Unfortunately, they don't have such items, and likely, you don't have them either.

Next do the same for expense below $200, $100, $50, and $20. Unless you have a lot, and I really mean *a lot*, of expenses below $20, there is no sense to go below this amount. Do the same on each level. Remember, the lower you get, the lower is effect. If you can cut $500 expense, you should do that, if you can cut $20 expense, it may be a good idea to cut it. See the difference?

Little hints

Again, you and only you can decide, what is important and what is not. But here are some hints to common unnecessary expenses.

Cable TV

Yes, usually you don't need one. In most areas you can have several public channels without a cable. And even if you don't, that's not the end of the world. Think, what will you miss with TV? News about disasters all over the world? Stupid cartoons? Boring movies? A lot of advertising? If you are so addicted to TV, rent a video. This way at least you will get the time spent for nothing under control, as well as what exactly you see.

Did you heard about the latest horror movie about the videotape, which killed everybody, who viewed it? Do you know, that this is really possible to create such a tape? Do you remember Pokemon serial, one of which series resulted in a lot of epileptic seizures across Japan? How hard do you think is to make such a tape and make it on air?

When you are shopping in a grocery store, you probably prefer juice not from concentrate, organically grown vegetables, and butter with less cholesterol. Right? You care about what you put inside your body. And you are right. But should not be you even more concerned about what you put inside your brain and soul?

Granted, cable TV is just 30-40 bucks a month. But that's still money, you can use better. Besides, what may be much more important, *time is money*, and you need money, remember? You need to work on the family budget, you need to get extra income. Can you spend the time better, than sitting on a coach and consuming, whatever some complete strangers want you to see and hear?

I am not saying that you should drop cable TV, it's up to you to decide. But I hope, that I gave you some material for a thought.

Expensive vacations

Vacation is essential. Without vacations you may work out yourself in the condition, where you will not be able to work. Getting annual rest and change of scenery lets you run.

But does it have to be expensive? Consider alternatives. Get a better travel agent, if you need one. Look for the deals on hotels and air planes. Use your car instead of a plane, if destination is reasonably close enough. And if it is not, may be you have some other place, not so far from you?

Is your dentist getting too much from you?

That's tough. When you talk to dentist, you may find out that you should clean your teeth four times a year, get a filling into each of them, then remove about half of them one by one to replace with dentures. After that you still have to clean the rest of them four times a year, fill cavities, and periodically remove some tooth to get new, even more expensive dentures.

Sounds familiar? Maybe not. Not all dentists are *so* greedy. But still there are reasonable bounds of what you really need and what you don't. My current family dentist insists that all members of my family should have four cleanings every year. Otherwise we all should lose all our teeth very soon, and become very pitiful creatures, who will require removal of lost teeth and dentures. I still wonder how lost teeth may require removal, but, hey, who would bother expert with such questions? However. my previous dentist, who is highly professional specialist in orthodontia, told me that every cleaning disturbing teeth and has a potential for new cavities. And I trust him. He removed a really bad tooth without painkillers so that I did not felt a thing. And after *his* cleaning I really felt a difference. So we don't have four cleaning per year, but just two. Guess what? All our teeth are still in place.

Again, that requires some homework and knowledge, because what have to be done, you want to be done. You want cavities filled, and your mouth healthy. But think. Is your dentist making something, you don't really need? After all you are the one, who is paying. And even if your insurance covers 80%, you still going to pay something substantial, you can use better.

Now do this!

Now put this book aside and do this. Yes, really!

Are you still reading? Get to the action, remember, reading does not help if you don't really *do*.

…(this is left intentionally empty to give you time to do something!)

Ok, you found some expenses, you are ready to cut. You still have not done so, but you are ready, and you are already suffering from absence of these things. Right? Yeah, that is tough. You feel deprived of something, you really have a right for. You may even feel your self a failure. "What, no cable TV for my family?!" Fine, calm down. Dealing with this stress is what we are getting to.

Compensating for cut items

Cutting expenses mean that you don't get something. Not surprisingly, it hurts. Some people, when trying to stop some expenses, really suffer and cannot tolerate that for long. What to do in this case.

Before we can get to how you can handle cutting expenses psychologically, let get to another question. Why would you suffer? Really, you just have decided that this is not essential. Why suffer about something nonessential? It's illogical. You can refer to the fact that human beings are illogical, and that's what often makes them human beings. This is true, but let dive deeper into what "illogical" means, and why humans are illogical, and you will see a plenty ways out of this problem.

Every human being is symbiosis of two parts, conscious mind and subconsciousness. When I type the last word Microsoft Word highlights word subconsciousness as a spelling error. That's because though the whole world knows about it, it's not so wide known in America. Even so, you are likely have heard this word before.

Your subconsciousness is like a little child within you. It's also like a woman to a man, subconsciousness always gets what it wants. So if you want something from yourself, you better make your subconsciousness want it. And if you will really want it, don't worry, whatever it is, you will do that.

The problem is that your subconsciousness is really like a little child, and it's mostly driven by your instincts. Mainly these are the two ones: self-preservation and procreation. Because it is like a child, you can distract its attention to substitutions, like art, poetry, and a lot of other things. By the way, one of them is making money. Such a distraction is called *sublimation*. Sublimation serves as a substitute to original things, when they are not easily available. The things, subconsciousness really wants.

As an example, why so many attempts to quit smoking fail? Why so many attempts to quit drinking fail? Why so many attempts to quit gambling fail? There is but one reason, because subconsciousness does not want that. It's very important part of you, and neglecting it will not bring you any good. It also does not bring you any good to deny that subconsciousness has such influence on you. Subconsciousness is like a steering wheel in the car. You can take a passenger seat, deny its role, and believe that your dreams make things happen, while letting your car drive into the nearest tree. Or, you can take a driver seat by making your subconsciousness want the same thing you want.

Simply put, if you ignore that, subconsciousness is what drives you, and your our conscious mind is a tool to satisfy these demands. If you are a spiritual person, subconsciousness becomes a tool for you to drive yourself to what you believe.

What it boils down to, is that though sublimation is possible and widespread, it's still is just a substitute. And those items, you had cut, are just a substitute to more basic things. Remember? Self-preservation and procreation. And so these substitute things can be easily substituted with the actual basic things.

Got it? Not yet? Ok, let me tell an anecdote. Do you know a French diet to keep the weight under control? Here it is.

Breakfast: cakes and sex. Lunch: cakes and sex. Dinner: cakes and sex. If it does not help, cut out cereal.

Got it? All your subconsciousness needs is self-preservation and procreation. Fear and love. Food, shelter, and intimacy. That's all your subconsciousness wants and needs from you to be happy. And when it is happy, you are free to do whatever you really want.

It's even better and worse at the same time, depending on if you are in a driver or passenger seat. These two things are what your subconsciousness uses as a bottom line to track your performance. If it's happy, it remembers what you are doing and making you do it again and again. If it's not, it makes you to stop doing, what you are doing now, and try something else. That's how sublimation gets into the picture in the first place! Sublimation activities are what your subconsciousness believes being successful in the past in bringing you these two basic things.

You see, whatever stupid thing you have to cut out, there is no reason to suffer. It is all replaceable with good food inside your home and love. Remember "Step minus one" in the beginning of this book? The golden rule is love. Romantic evening with a small amount of tasty food, sweet talk, and passionate conclusion is a sure shot recipe to forget about missing cable TV and other stupid and expensive stuff.

A little religious digression

If you are not religious, better just skip this part. You are likely to be annoyed, and if not, you will get a bunch of interesting, but not very useful for you facts. If you are, read on. You could find something both interesting, motivating, and useful for you.

You may feel a bit shocked by so Freudian and earthly approach as described above. Don't be. There is a great deal of spirituality inside all this. Let look in the Bible, namely look into Genesis, the story of how man and woman were created, and how they've got themselves out of heavens. Modern translation bring a lot of confusion into this story, because in the original Hebrew text the same word םדא [ad'am] mean at the same time human, man, and Adam (KJV "Ad'am"). Therefore translations use these three words often in arbitrary order and obfuscate the meaning of the story.

What's the difference between these word and how to draw the line, where each of them are really meant to be? "Adam" is a proper name of the person, who was the first man. That's it. "Man" is a male human. And "human", whether man or a woman, is the creation of God made in His image. To understand what is meant there, let look how words "woman" and "Eva" (we follow spelling and text of the King James version in this book.) Look at the Genesis 3:20, "And Ad'am called his wife's name Eve…" That happens when they are sent out of heaven for their sin. Before, in heaven, she was just "woman." Did you ever thought why? The same verse answers that question, "…because she was the mother of all living." In other words, after that event an existence of other female human beings become possible. So she got a proper name to be distinct from her daughters and female descendants.

Now, let's return to the man. Some translations get it right, when they introduce the proper name "Adam" immediately after the woman was created. But why? Why not at the same time as Eva got her name? After all, this is the time when the possibility of other human beings, male or female, appeared. Should the same logic applicable to a woman, be applicable to the man?

The answer is simple. Before woman was created the word סדא [ad'am] (Adam, man, human) was used in the meaning "human." After that he become man as opposed to a "woman" and to distinct between them two. And when the woman become "Eva", he actually become "Adam", the person who was the first male human being, distinct from all other male human beings originated from him.

King James version says:

"And the Lord God, caused a deep sleep to fall upon Ad'am, and he slept: and he took one of his ribs, and closed up the flesh instead thereof; And the rib, which the Lord God had taken from man, made he a woman, and brought her unto the man." (Gen 3:21-22)

Let notice the word "rib." Actually this is a word עלצ [tse'la], which mean not only "rib", but also "side." What God took from the first human being was *his female side*. What was left, that is male side, became a man.

If we will read the same verses with these two corrections in mind, it will say: "And the Lord God, caused a deep sleep to fall upon *human*, and he slept: and he took one of his *sides*, and closed up the flesh instead thereof; And the *side*, which the Lord God had taken from *human*, made he a *woman*, and brought her unto the *man*."

Therefore it's not *man*, it's *human*, which was created in God's image:

"And God said, Let us make man *in our image*, after our likeness: and let them have dominion over the fish of the sea, and over the fowl of the air, and over the cattle, and *over all the earth*, and over every creeping thing that creepth upon the earth." (Genesis, 1:26)

You may be interested to reread the next verse in the light of what was described above:

"So God created man *in his own image*, in the *image of God* created he him; *male and female* created he them." (Genesis 1:27)

Now, with everything in place, you should see that you are just a half of human, whether male or female. Only together you make the whole. Only together you make the whole human being, which was created in God's image and which was made the master of all Earth with the power to create and change things. The power to change any things, including your financial status. Hey, remember "Step minus One"?

So what your subconsciousness wants is to make you whole and powerful. That's it. Do you still think that this is Freudian and earthly?

Well, being whole is good, but sex is often considered a sin, right? So how it could be good? Yes, it can! That's just another mistake commonly in place, which pollute consciousness of many people. You see, reading the Bible or other holy scriptures is a laborious job. You cannot arbitrary take what you want and discard, what you don't. Let take one of the commandments, for example:

"Six days shalt thou labor, and do all thy work: But the seventh day is the Sabbath of the Lord thy God: in it thou shalt not do any work..." (Exodus 20:9-10)

On numerous occasions this commandment was read only from one side. Some see that you *should not work* on the seventh day. Some see that you *should work* six days, and often "six days" get lost. The second case is a common sin in America, when people continue to work through weekend without leaving themselves any chance to rest. You see, actually this commandment requires both that you do work six days, and actually "do *all* thy work", as well as that you "shalt not do any work" on the seventh day.

The same thing is often happening to sex. Outside of marriage it is a sin, and this is said on numerous occasions in many holy texts. But inside marriage it is not a sin, it's required, it's one of the things people *should* do. See for yourself:

"Therefore shall a man leave his father and his mother, and shall cleave unto his wife: and they shall be one flesh." (Genesis 3:24)

And Jesus enforced that with his:

"Wherefore they are no more twain, but one flesh. What therefore God hath joined together, let not man put asunder." (Matt. 19:6)

If you will apply the rule of both sides, you will see that the Bible is very clear on this subject. Thou shalt not commit sex outside of marriage. Thou shalt do sex in marriage.

If you want to go even deeper, "Thou shalt not commit adultery." (Exod. 20:14, Matt. 5:27, Matt. 19:18) is actually talking not just about sex outside marriage, but much more. The word used for "adultery" generally is interpreted in the original texts as "improper connection", "getting together something that should be apart." That's the real sin, which our Dark Ages ancestors mistakenly interpreted as just relations between man and woman.

Step 9: Getting shopping controllable

Budget expenses

Early of later we had to come to this. See what money you have for the items, you are usually buying. Plan only what's necessary. And then stick to the plan. Don't buy on spot, even if it looks like a great deal.

What's really important, is that you separated money, you can spend on regular needs, like food and household items, and you spend just that. For the hints on how to actually do this see right below.

Use cash or ATM card from a special account for store shopping

One way is to use cash, and not carry a credit card with you. Estimate what you can spend per day, and have just this amount with you. This way you can spend only what you can afford. Of course, no technique is foolproof, and I mean each part of this word, but often this helps, I know some families, which follow this practice for years.

Another way is to get monthly or semi-monthly expenses onto a separate account, and use ATM card from this account. This also limits your expenses in some degree. However, what will you do, if you will spend the whole amount on the first day? As you see, this method requires more self-control than cash.

Shopping list

A good idea is to have family shopping list. When anybody in the family thinks that something should be bought, he should right it down into the shopping list. Everything more that certain amount should be approved by family. It's up to you, what should be the limit, but there is no sense to keep it too low. Many people use $50 threshold for that.

Now when you are going to some store, you are buying by the list, and never anything, which is not in the list. If you have seen something, you want, get home and include it into the shopping list. Never buy on a spot. You will be surprised, how much this simple trick can do to your budget.

Are you impulsive buyer?

Here comes a good one. A lot of people are impulsive buyers. That means that to the contrary to advice above, they do buy on a spot. If this is the case, it is usually a huge sinkhole for family money.

In fact, this is so common problem, that you may see articles on this topic. With the "convenience" of credit cards, this is a huge problem for many families. So how to avoid that? For regular stores, shopping list can help a lot. That is if you can resist temptation.

Close channels: store shopping, Internet, TV ads, mail order

Try to find out, where you are most prone to impulsive shopping? In a physical store? On the Internet? In front of TV? Browsing through a mail order catalog?

Find the most dangerous channels, and close them. Just don't look into mail order catalog, or stop using Internet, or at least sites like eBay. If you cannot stop that, try shopping list approach. If this does not help, but you still need to buy something there, let your spouse handle that shopping. That is if he or she is better than you at controlling shopping urges.

In hard cases, close all your credit cards.

Step 10: Budgeting food?

Not likely

If you are not hooked on outside meals, it's unlikely, that you can get much from budgeting food expenses. United States is a relatively cheap country when it comes to food. Cheap relatively to average salary, of course, it's not easy to beat actual prices somewhere in Greece or Spain.

Still there are some things, you can try. Normally this will not give you much effect, but if you have certain problems, it may help.

Do not waste

How much of the products, do you have to throw away? How much products you keep in refrigerator at the same time? How much fruits and vegetables rot on your kitchen table, while waiting to be consumed?

I don't even mention, that with most of the world starving, this is just immoral to waste products. That is also money, which you lost for nothing.

The recipe to handle this problem is actually pretty easy. Don't buy reserves. Have enough food in the house for a couple of days. If you are afraid of emergencies, buy some canned food, and put it away. Don't forget to eat it some time later, and replace with the fresh one.

Before going to a store, ask yourself, do you really need to go there, or you have enough food in the house? Never go to the store if you have enough in the house for several days (not considering emergency rations.) If you still have to, because you are missing some essential ingredient, buy just this ingredient, nothing else. Don't take a cart, better don't take even basket. If you need just one item, your hands are enough.

When buying food, ask yourself, when you are going to eat it? Today? Tomorrow? In three-four days? In a week? In last cases, can you buy it later? Can the product survive until the planned day?

Be honest with yourself. Can you really eat tomorrow four pounds of beef, four pounds of pork, and four pounds of chicken? Maybe your whole family can, but will it do them any good? Don't double book your meals. If you do that unconsciously, make menu ahead for several days, so that you know exactly what you are buying and for which meal.

Again stick to the shopping list, don't buy anything, which is not on the list. If the list is short enough, don't use a cart. Shopping cart is a great temptation, a single item look so lonely inside, that it's just uncomfortable.

If you still wasted some product, buy less of it next time. Yes, it's a great temptation to buy an "economy" pack. But think why "economy" packs are cheaper per pound? This is because you buy more, because you end up spending more money. If something is going away from your fridge quickly, you can buy in relatively large quantities. Say at Costco or Sam's club. But if something had rotten, you need less of it. Or maybe you just should not buy things, which end up in the trash.

Family meals

Making one dinner for four is much cheaper, simpler, and faster than making four individual dinners for each member of the family. Your kids may think that family dinners are not cool. That's fine, you can survive that. And they will survive family dinners as well.

Of course, that may require some discipline. And that's not easy. But you can do that. One common problem in getting this done, is the presence of snacks in the house. Remember what we were talking about fast food? Snacks are a home-based equivalent of fast food. Don't buy them. After kids get a snack, it's very hard to make them eat. Then you will think that they are hungry, and all your efforts will go nowhere.

Great dinners for under $1.75 per person

If you wonder, how much you need to feed the family, look into appendix. You will find there a month of dinners under $7 for four people. That is below $1.75 per person. Each dinner includes a salad and a main dish. The main dish is normally under $5, that is $1.25 per person!

Most recipes are very simple, and can be prepared by even by a beginner without much hassle. And a whole month of recipes guarantees that your dinners will have a nice variety, so you don't have to worry that somebody will get bored with a particular dish.

Step 11: Can you utilize an existing asset?

Your main income

Can you increase your main income? Usually the answer is no. To start from, at least one of you already have a job, and the salary is exactly what is not sufficient to sustain your family budget. Let's be honest with ourselves, promotion is not likely, and salary increases even in best times were not so high to cover your deficit. Unless, of course, it is very small, in which case you can easily fix it by cutting few expenses.

It is important to notice, that performance review is not the only way to increase your salary. Changing jobs may be able to help with that too. It is also important to remember, that the time for now are different from 90s. Jobs are scarce and hiring companies are more hesitant to offer more that you had before. In fact, people, who already lost their jobs and found another, often have done so with a pay cut. So, before doing anything in this direction, it's worth to think a lot first.

So, why have I mentioned this first? Because even though salary increase is not likely to happen and is not likely to resolve your problems, this is still your main income. Keep this in mind, and don't jeopardize it in the process of trying to get more income.

Professional job

If one of you does not have a job, can he or she get one? Yes, that's not easy, but it's important to try. Second professional income will help you a lot, and actually will take you out of financial trouble, unless your spending habits are hopelessly expensive.

We are talking here about professional income. If you have a profession, try to get a job matching your skills. Sometimes it may look like impossible task, but ask yourself a simple question. How high is the chance that you will do nothing and the job will find you?

In my case, like with most people, this is highly unlikely. Do you know what is the difference between winners and losers? Loser actions are described by a row:

…lose, lose, lose, lose, lose, quit.

Winner actions are like:

…lose, WIN!

This fact is recognized by people of all times across the globe. A Roman would say "ex nihil, nihil fit", that is "nothing comes from nothing." I will not bore you with hundreds of proverbs and phrases, saying the same thing in all languages and in all alphabets, and cut directly to the American one: "Winners never quit, quitters never win."

Make it your mantra. Repeat it several times a day. Print and put on the wall, where you will see it. And continue your attempts until you will succeed.

Non-professional job?

Sales associate in a department store, cashier at a gas station, janitor, pizza delivery, sandwich assembler at McDonald. Even in current times there is abundance of low-paid grossly unsatisfactory jobs, which nobody really wants, but many have to take. If you don't have a job, and have not followed advice above or have no profession from the beginning, consider these opportunities. After all, your task is to cover deficit or at least slow down fall, right?

Don't expect much from these jobs. Full time $7 per hour job makes 40*$7 = $280 per week before taxes, or a bit more than $1000 per month before taxes. And you know what this black magic word "before taxes" can do to your income.

So even if you had to take such a job, never stop to look for a better paid one. If you don't have a profession, do your best to get one. If you have, continue to search for the professional high-paid job.

Notice, that taking such low-paid jobs is not free. If it is full-time, it's hard to hide it, and it will be tough to explain such job on your professional resume. If it has health benefit, you may have to take a much worse medical insurance from such job, instead of a better insurance provided by your spouse employer. This can easily result in higher medical expenses.

Don't make a mistake, this is only an option if you don't have a lot of other options. If you either take the job, or declare yourself bankrupt next month. If you are so beaten up, that you are not trying anymore. If you hide in your shell and afraid of outside world, so that it keeps you from getting a real job. But in these cases, this is an option.

Irregular or one-time income?

Surprisingly, irregular income is much less damaging and often much more rewarding than low-paid jobs. Most of opportunities for such income come from independent sales in one form or another. There is a number of jobs, which require relatively little formal training, but may be very rewarding in a case of success. By "relatively", I mean that you don't need a 6-year college degree to work there and training expenses are reasonable. Among these jobs are:

- insurance agent

- real estate agent

- mortgage broker

Most of these jobs require some license, so you often have to start as an assistant of some licensed professional. However in a case of success even single sale may bring substantial money.

Less profitable is commission-based telemarketing or other sales, including legitimate forms of multi-level marketing. These jobs require even less initial investment, and also may result in a great success, if the company and the product are right, and you are smart and persistent.

In your own professional area, you can try contracting. In a case of success, even one time project may help you substantially. And with experience, you will get more.

All these jobs are more entrepreneur style and business, rather than jobs. And all of them don't look reliable to people accustomed to a pay-check. But if you dare to cross the line, if you smart and persistent, and if you have selected the type of business right, it may be better than regular paycheck. And if you don't have a job anyway, and you live on your spouse's salary, what's keeping you up?

Beside such irregular income jobs, there are one time opportunities. For example, you may not plan to go into contracting, but opportunity just happen. Say, friend of your friend needs some work done, which you can do. Go for it! You will feel much better, and even one time income helps a lot. Sometimes such accidental income may be enough to supplement your spouse salary and can keep you afloat.

Step 12: Can you acquire or create new assets?

Until now we were talking about *jobs*. However, remember that we started from assets? Do you remember what is asset? That's something that brings you money.

Assets normally work for you, instead of you working for money. For example, having a second house and renting it, gives you an income. In essence this is like the old game Monopoly. But assets are more than real estate. It can be money on your account, which pays interest. It can be share in some business. It can be patent or copyright for a work, which brings money. For example, Dilbert character is an asset of Scott Adams.

Assets are much better than just source of income like salary, because while it works for you, you can normally do something else.

Can you somehow acquire assets, which will bring you extra income? Can you create some asset, which will bring you extra income?

This step is intentionally so short. If you dare to go here, there is a huge ocean of materials, books, tapes, and seminars, which will help you on your journey. Bon voyage and good luck!

Epilogue

This book is over. Ok, it is not completely over, there are still dinner recipes for a whole month. But the part about managing family finances is over. However, your work is just started. Remember, there is only one way to get success. That is by actually doing them.

No matter how good the book is, you and only you are the one, who will resolve your problem and succeed. Good luck!

Appendix: A month of great dinners for under $1.75 per person

So, how much should a meal cost? The right answer is "very little." Let's start from the breakfasts.

Breakfasts

Modern cereal breakfast

A $4 box of cereal is normally enough for about 7 breakfasts. That is 58¢ per serving. A gallon of milk costs around $2.50 and contains 16 half-pint cups. That is 16¢ per cup. The whole breakfast is:

Cereal	58¢
Milk	16¢
Total	74¢

Traditional cooked breakfast

A pound of pasta costs 70¢ and makes enough for four people. That is 18¢ per serving. A pound of margarine costs 90¢ and contains about 40 teaspoons. That is about 3¢ per teaspoon. A teabag sold in a $3 box of 200 bags costs about 2¢. An 8-pack of generic hot dogs is easily available for $1.50. That is 38¢ per two hot dogs. To account water and salt you need a cheaper currency then dollars and cents. The whole breakfast is:

Pasta	18¢
Margarine	3¢
Two hot dogs	38¢
Cup of Lipton "Brisk" tea	2¢
Total	61¢

Replacing pasta with dried mashed potatoes or rice does not change the picture significantly.

James Bond breakfast

Two dozen eggs cost $2.99 at Costco, 12¢ per egg. A pack of about a dozen slices of bacon can be found for $2, 16¢ per slice. Margarine is calculated above. The whole breakfast is:

Two eggs	24¢
Two slices of bacon	33¢
Margarine	3¢
Cup of English tea	5¢
Total	65¢

"On the run" sandwich breakfast

Bread for 99¢ contains more than 30 slices, that is 7¢ per two slices. A pack of 10-20 slices of bologna costs about $2.50, 25¢ per slice. A pound cheese costs about $5 and makes 10 thick slices, 50¢ per slice. A $3 pack of greenery from Costco is enough for a lot of sandwiches, but you also eat things you do not necessarily put into the sandwich, so let's assume it provides for 20 sandwiches, 15¢ a sandwich. At last, a two-liter Coke bottle can be found for $1.00 and contains about 8 glasses, 13¢ per glass. The total is:

Two slices of bread	7¢
Two slices of bologna	50¢
One thick slice of cheese	50¢
Green salad	15¢
Glass of Coke	13¢
Total	$1.35

No big surprise there, unhealthy food is almost always more expensive.

Lunches

Most people have lunch at work, but you always can take it with you. In this case, lunch may not be much different from the traditional cooked breakfast described above. That is mere 61¢! Even with variations, it will rarely cost more that $1.

Dinners

Below you will find 31 dinners for every day of the month, dinners that are easy to cook, healthy, tasty, and cost less than $1.75 per person. That is less than $7 for a family of four.

We did not try to make it as cheap as possible, and finding a cheaper dinner is not a problem. For example, you can take a traditional cooked breakfast, described above, and add a cup of chicken broth that costs 50¢, making the whole dinner just $1.11 per person.

How cheap can it be? The question is not very practical, but how about pasta cooked in a chicken broth made out of dried cubes? Here are the calculations:

Pasta	18¢
Bouillon cube	10¢
Cup of tea	2¢
Total	30¢

Note that 18¢ of pasta is not a "cup of noodles", but much more and much better. In a dry state, it is a quarter of a pound. After it is cooked, it's likely to be over a pound of ready pasta.

Of course, this is a bit extreme, but worth it to know. At least you will be honest, and will not torture yourself thinking that you deprive yourself of food by spending "a miserable $1.75" per meal. $1.75 is not the low end, and it is not even close to the really cheap food.

So here is the healthy, but still inexpensive alternative.

Day 1

Salad: Fresh Salad with Tomato and Cucumber

Serves 4

Ingredients:

3 large ripe tomatoes in medium dice

1 peeled cucumber, cut in half lengthwise and thinly sliced

1 tbsp light sour cream, or plain yogurt, or vegetable oil

Salt

Method:

Mix and salt to taste.

Remark:

This salad is a base for other salads. You can add diced celery, diced bell peppers, watercress, finely chopped shallot, torn and assorted salad greens such as romaine, mixed greens, peeled and diced apple and others. So, you will have dozens of different salads.

Price for 4 servings:

Tomatoes	$1.00
Cucumber	$0.70
Dressing	$0.10
Total:	$1.80

Day 1

Main dish: Grilled Salmon with Mashed potato

Serves 4

Ingredients

1 small onion, chopped

1 lb fish fillets

1 lb potato

3 tbsp vegetable oil

2 tbsp lemon juice

Salt, pepper, seasoning mix to taste

Method

Place the potatoes in a large pan of lightly salted water. Bring to a boil and cook for 20 minutes. Drain the potato and place in a blender or in a food processor fitted with a metal blade. Add the sour cream, 1/2 teaspoon salt, 1/4 teaspoon ground pepper and hot water or non-fat milk. Process or blend on high speed just until it becomes smooth and creamy, which is about 20 seconds. Add the vegetable oil and blend for another 15 seconds to combine. Taste and adjust the seasoning. Set aside, covered.

In a small skillet, heat the oil, add the onion, and cook for 3 minutes. Set aside and keep warm while you cook the fish. Meanwhile, sprinkle both sides of the salmon fillets with salt, lemon juice and grounded pepper to taste. Grill the fish fillets over high heat, or place under a broiler for 4 to 5 minutes on each side, depending on the thickness of the fish, until the salmon is firm, pale pink and opaque throughout when flaked with a fork. Place the mashed potatoes in serving plates and top with the fillets. Sprinkle each plate with an equal amount of the cooked onion and serve immediately.

Price for 4 servings:

Salmon	$4.00
Potato	$0.70
Dressing	$0.30
Total	$5.00

Day 2

Salad: Fresh salad with radish

Serves 4

Ingredients:

1 cup thinly sliced radish,

4 cups torn salad greens,

2 tbsp finely chopped green onions

1 tbsp vegetable oil, salt, sugar, 1 tsp lemon juice or vinegar

Method:

For dressing: stir together the oil, lemon juice, salt and sugar

For salad: In a large salad bowl, combine the salad greens, radish, and onions. Drizzle the dressing over the top and shake gently to mix.

Price for 4 servings:

Radish	$0.50
Salad greens	$0.80
Green onions	$0.10
Dressing	$0.20
Total:	$1.60

Day 2

Main dish: Beef Casserole

Serves 4

Ingredients:

1 1/2 pounds beef chuck, trimmed of all fat and cut into 1 1/2- inch cubes

2 medium onions, peeled and chopped

3 medium carrots, peeled, cut into 1/4-inch slices, or grated

1/2 cup all-purpose flour, 1/2 tablespoon salt, 1 tbsp freshly ground black pepper

2 tablespoons vegetable oil, 1/2 cup dry red wine (or red wine vinegar), 1/2 cups beef broth or stock, seasoning to taste

Method:

In a large saucepan over medium-high heat, warm the oil; add the onions and sauté, turning frequently until brown on all sides (about 5-6 minutes). Remove the onions with a slotted spoon.

In a large bowl, mix together the flour, salt, and pepper. Add the beef and coat evenly with the seasoned flour. Cook the beef in the fat that remains in the pan, stirring frequently, until the beef is brown evenly on all sides (about 5 minutes). Add the wine, broth, and carrots. Return the onions to the pan. Stir thoroughly and bring the mixture to a simmer. Reduce the heat to medium, cover, and simmer until the beef is tender (about 1 hour). Taste and adjust the seasonings, if necessary. Serve the stew over the hot noodles, potato, rice, or another garnish.

Price for 4 servings:

Beef	$4.00
Carrots	$0.30
Onion	$0.20
Flour	$0.10
Beef broth	$0.20
Red wine	$0.10
Oil, salt, pepper	$0.10
Total:	$5.00

Day 3

Salad: Fresh salad with apple and radish

Serves 4

Ingredients:

3 large peeled, seeded, then diced apples

1 cup of chopped radish

1 tbsp of light sour cream, or plain yogurt

Salt and sugar to taste.

Method:

Mix apples, radish, and yogurt. Season with salt and sugar.

Price for 4 servings:

Apples	$1.00
Radish	$0.50
Dressing	$0.10
Total:	$1.60

Day 3

Main dish: Fish and Potato Bake

Serves 4

Ingredients:

1 medium onion, chopped

1 lb fish fillets

1 lb potato, peeled, cooked and sliced

3 tbsp vegetable oil

1 cup milk, 2 eggs

Salt, pepper

Method:

In a small skillet, heat the oil, add the onion, and cook for 3 minutes.

Set aside and keep warm while you cook the fish.

Sprinkle both sides of the fish fillets with salt, lemon juice and grounded pepper to taste, then dip them into flour to coat evenly.

Heat the oil in a large pan to 350F, place the fish fillets, and cook for 4 to 5 minutes on each side (depending on the thickness of the fish) until the fish is ready.

Place the sliced potatoes over the fillets. Sprinkle with the cooked onion. Pour a mix of the milk and eggs into the pan over the fish and vegetables, and bake until ready.

Price for 4 servings:

Fish	$4.00
Potato	$0.30
Onion	$0.20
Flour	$0.10
Eggs	$0.20
Milk	$0.10
Oil, salt, pepper	$0.10
Total:	$5.00

Day 4

Salad: Fresh salad with cabbage

Serves 4

Ingredients:

    1 lb of thinly sliced cabbage

    2 tbsp finely chopped shallot or another green onion

    2 tbsp finely chopped dill

    2 tbsp vegetable oil

    2 tbsp vinegar

    Salt, sugar to taste

Method:

For dressing: Stir vegetable oil, vinegar and sugar

For salad: In a large salad bowl, combine the cabbage and salt and knead by hands. Add shallot and dill to the bowl, stir, add the dressing and stir well.

Price for 4 servings:

Cabbage	$0.70
Green onion	$0.30
Dill	$0.50
Dressing	$0.10
Total:	$1.60

Day 4

Main dish: Beef Stroganoff

Serves 4

Ingredients:

1 pound beef tenderloin cut into 1/2-inch strips

1 large onion

1/2 cup sliced mushrooms

1 tbsp butter

1 tbsp vegetable oil

2 tbsp all-purpose flour

1 cup beef broth or water

1 tbsp Dijon mustard

2 tbsp sour cream

Salt, paprika, and freshly ground black pepper to taste

Method:

In a large, heavy sauté pan, heat the oil over medium-high heat. Add the beef and sauté, stirring frequently for 4 to 6 minutes until just cooked. Remove the beef, and drain on the paper towels.

Melt the butter in the same sauté pan. Add the onions and mushrooms. Cook, stirring frequently, until the onions are translucent (about 5 minutes). Sprinkle the flour over the onion-mushroom mixture. Stir well and cook for 3 minutes.

Stir in the beef broth or water and bring the mixture to a boil. Stir in the mustard, pepper, salt, and paprika. Return the beef to the pan. Cover and simmer until the beef is tender (about 5 minutes).

Stir in the sour cream. Serve beef Stroganoff over hot noodles, potatoes, or rice.

Price for 4 servings:

Beef	$3.40
Mushrooms	$0.80
Onion	$0.20
Flour	$0.10
Beef broth	$0.40
Sour cream, butter	$0.20
Oil, salt, pepper, mustard	$0.10
Total:	$5.00

Day 5

Salad: Tomatoes and onions salad

Serves 4

Ingredients:

4 large ripe tomatoes in medium dice

1 large finely chopped onion

1 tbsp vegetable oil

Salt

Method:

Mix the ingredients, and season with salt to taste.

Remark: This salad is a base for other salads. You can add diced celery, diced bell pepper, watercress, torn assorted salad greens, mixed greens, and shredded cheese. And, of course, you can use different dressings. So, you will have dozens of different salads.

Price for 4 servings:

Tomatoes	$1.20
Sweet onion	$0.30
Dressing	$0.10
Total:	$1.60

Day 5

Main dish: Vegetable cutlets

Serves 4

Ingredients:

2 lbs potato, peeled, and cooked

2 eggs

1/2 cup all-purpose flour

1 large onion, finely chopped

2 tbsp vegetable oil

Salt, pepper, and seasoning to taste

Method:

Drain the potato and place in a blender or in a food processor fitted with a metal blade. Add 1 tbsp vegetable oil, 1/2 tsp salt, and flour. Process or blend on a high speed just until smooth and creamy (about 20 seconds). Add the eggs and blend for another 20 seconds to combine. Taste and adjust the seasoning.

In a large skillet, heat the oil, and cook over medium heat for 4 to 5 minutes on each side, depending on the thickness of the potato cutlets.

Note: You may cook the vegetable cutlets from any vegetable or mix of vegetables.

Price for 4 servings:

Potato	$1.20
Onion	$0.30
Flour	$0.10
Oil and spices	$0.10
Total:	$1.70

Day 6

Salad: Cucumber Salad

Serves 4

Ingredients:

2 cucumbers, peeled, thinly sliced

2 tablespoons chopped fresh dill

Salt to taste

2 tbsp of your favorite dressing

Method:

In a mixing bowl, combine the cucumber, dill and dressing. Mix gently, add salt and stir.

Remark: This salad is a base for other salads. You can add parsley, onions, basilicas, diced celery, diced bell pepper, watercress, torn assorted salad greens, mixed greens, shredded cheese and so on. You can use different dressings. So, you will have tens of different salads.

Price for 4 servings:

Cucumber	$1.00
Dill	$0.50
Dressing	$0.30
Total:	$1.80

Day 6

Main dish: Baked squash with a meat stuffing

Serves 4

Ingredients:

4 small acorn squash

4 medium onion, finely chopped

4 garlic cloves, crushed

2 tbsp vegetable oil

4 tbsp mixed spices (ginger, coriander, chili powder, etc.)

3 cup minced pork or beef

1 tbsp chopped parsley

Salt and pepper to taste

Optional, for stuffing: cooked rice, peeled and chopped tomatoes, grated hard-cook eggs, grated cheese, etc.)

Method:

Preheat the oven to 400 degrees F. Cut off the top of the squash and scoop out the seeds, keep the tops. Cut a slice off the bases of the squash so the shells can stand upright on a baking sheet.

Gently fry the onions and garlic in the oil in a frying pan until they begin to brown. Add the spices to the pan and fry, stirring constantly, for about 1 minute. Add the pork and fry until the meat has browned (about 7 minutes). Stir in the parsley. Season to taste. Remove from the heat and spoon the meat stuffing into the center of each squash until firmly packed. Replace the lids on the squash and cook on the middle shelf of the oven for 1 hour, or until the squash are soft and cooked through and the stuffing is piping hot. Serve with hot noodles or rice.

Price for 4 servings:

Meat	$3.00
Squash	$1.00
Onion	$0.50
Vegetable oil	$0.10
Parsley, garlic	$0.20
Spices	$0.20
Total:	$5.00

Day 7

Salad: Fresh bell pepper and tomato salad

Serves 4

Ingredients:

- 1 red bell pepper, seeded and finely chopped
- 1 green bell pepper, seeded and finely chopped
- 2 tomatoes, coarsely chopped
- 1 tablespoon red wine vinegar
- 1/5 teaspoon salt
- 1-tablespoon vegetable oil
- 1 tablespoon chopped fresh parsley

Method:

In a bowl, mix together all the ingredients.

Price for 4 servings:

Red bell pepper	$0.80
Green bell pepper	$0.70
Tomatoes	$0.50
Parsley	$0.10
Dressing	$0.10
Total:	$2.20

Day 7

Main dish: Boiled potato with a mushroom stuffing

Serves 4

Ingredients:

4 large potato, peeled and washed

1/2 lb champignons

2 peaces any white bread

2 large onion, finely chopped

1 egg

1 tbsp butter

1 tbsp sour cream

Salt, pepper to taste

Method:

Cut off the top of the potato and scoop out the center. Keep the tops. In a pot, bring water to a boil. Add salt and mushrooms. Cook until ready. Drain the mushrooms; keep the stock. In a large pan, gently fry the onions in the oil until beginning to brown. Place the mushrooms, the onions, the bread and the egg in a food processor or in a blender. Process or blend on high speed for about 20 seconds. Taste and adjust the seasoning. Spoon the stuffing into the center of each potato until firmly packed. Replace the lids on the potato. Place potato in a pot; pour a mix of the mushroom stock and sour cream over the potato, and cook until ready (about 25 minutes over medium heat).

Note: You can coat the potato by a mix of mayonnaise and mustard then bake on the middle shelf of a medium heat oven for 40 minutes. Or, you can simmer it in a closed pot with 4 tbsp of mushroom stock.

You can use your favorite stuffing instead of the mushroom one.

Price for 4 servings:

Potato	$1.20
Onion	$0.30
Mushrooms	$1.50
Egg	$0.10
Butter, sour cream	$0.30
Bread	$0.10
Total:	$3.50

Day 8

Salad: Fresh salad with cabbage, carrot and apple

Serves 4

Ingredients:

1 lb of thinly sliced cabbage

1 medium sweet onion, thinly sliced

1 peeled, seeded and chopped apple

1 peeled and grated carrot

1/2-cup light sour cream or yogurt

2 tbsp vinegar

Salt, sugar, ground black pepper to taste

Method:

For dressing: Stir the light sour cream or yogurt, pepper and sugar

For salad: In a large microwave-safe bowl, combine the cabbage, vinegar and salt, then heat for 2 min. Chill. Add carrot and apple to the bowl, stir, add the dressing and stir well.

Price for 4 servings:

Cabbage	$0.70
Apple	$0.20
Carrot	$0.20
Dressing	$0.50
Total:	$1.60

Day 8

Main dish: Beef simmered with pepper

Serves 4

Ingredients:

1 pound beef tenderloin, cut into 1-inch strips

1/2 lb onion, finely chopped

1 cup white vinegar or white dry wine

1/2 lb tomato, peeled and diced

2 tbsp vegetable oil

Salt, paprika, and hot red pepper to taste

Method:

In a large, heavy sauté pan, heat the oil over medium-high heat. Add the onions and sauté, stirring frequently, 4 to 6 minutes until just browned. Add the beef and tomatoes; stir well. Cook about 5 minutes, stirring frequently. Stir in the pepper, salt, vinegar, and paprika. Cover and simmer for about 30 minutes.

Serve simmered beef over hot noodles, mashed potato, kasha, or rice.

Price for 4 servings:

Meat	$2.50
Tomato	$1.00
Onion	$0.40
Vegetable oil	$0.10
Spices	$0.20
Total:	$5.00

Day 9

Salad: Salad with tomatoes and cheese

Serves 4

Ingredients:

1 lb of peeled, seeded, and diced tomatoes

1 cup grated cheese

1/2-cup light mayonnaise or your favorite dressing

1 large garlic clove, peeled and minced

Salt, ground pepper to taste

Method:

In a salad bowl, combine the tomatoes, cheese and dressing, stir well. Add to bowl salt, garlic and ground pepper, stir well.

Price for 4 servings:

Tomato	$1.30
Cheese	$0.40
Garlic	$0.20
Dressing	$0.20
Total:	$2.10

Day 9

Main dish: Hot pot

Serves 4

Ingredients:

1 lb any meat, cut into 1-inch cubes

1 lb potato, peeled, washed and cut into 1-inch cubes

1 cup any stock

1 tbsp vegetable oil, salt and spices to taste

Optional ingredients:

1 lb any vegetables or vegetable mix, peeled and diced

4 tbsp sour cream, 1/2 lb any mushrooms, 1 large onion, salt, and greens to taste

Method:

In a large, heavy sauté pan, heat the oil over medium-high heat.

Add the meat and sauté, stirring frequently, 4 to 6 minutes until just brown.

Add the potato, stir well, and cook for 3-4 minutes.

Optional: In a large pan, heat the oil; fry the onions, vegetable, and mushrooms until beginning to brown. Add spices and sour cream to the pan and fry, stirring constantly, for about 1 minute. Add fried vegetables and mushrooms over the meat and the potato into a sauté pan.

Add a stock into the sauté pan. Cover and simmer for about 25 minutes.

Price for 4 servings:

Meat	$3.00
Potato	$0.60
Stock	$0.20
Vegetable oil	$0.10
Total:	$3.80

Day 10

Salad: Fresh salad with cabbage, tomato and cucumber

Serves 4

Ingredients:

1 lb thinly sliced cabbage

1 seeded and diced tomato

1 medium finely chopped cucumber

1 thinly sliced sweet onion

1 tbsp vegetable oil

Ground black pepper and mayonnaise to taste

Method:

In a salad bowl, stir all ingredients.

Price for 4 servings:

Cabbage	$0.70
Tomato	$0.30
Cucumber	$0.60
Onion	$0.30
Dressing	$0.10
Total:	$2.00

Day 10

Main dish: Baked potato with a cottage cheese

Serves 4

Ingredients:

4 large potato, washed

1/2 lb cottage cheese

1 bunch green onion, finely chopped

4 tbsp dill, parsley and other greens, finely chopped and mixed

4 tbsp sour cream

Salt, ground black pepper to taste

Method:

Wrap potatoes with a foil; lift the potato onto a baking sheet, and bake until ready, for about 1 hour over 400 degrees F. Meanwhile, place the cottage cheese, the greens, the salt, and the pepper in a food processor or in a blender. Process or blend on high speed for about 20 seconds. Taste, and if necessary, adjust the seasoning. Unfold the potatoes. Make the cuts on them, spoon the mix into the cut of each potato until firmly packed. Fold the potatoes with a foil. Place them in an oven, and cook until ready (about 5-7 minutes over medium heat). Then, unfold. Place on the plates, sprinkle with sour cream, and garnish with green onions and other greens.

Note: If you prefer, any root vegetables may be baked instead.

Price for 4 servings:

Potato	$1.20
Onion	$0.50
Cottage cheese	$1.50
Greens	$0.40
Sour cream	$0.40
Salt, pepper, seasoning	$0.20
Total:	$4.20

Day 11

Salad: Salad with corn and vegetables

Serves 4

Ingredients:

1 lb boiled cut corn

1/2-lb boiled in salted water cauliflower, cut into small florets

1 cup finely chopped peeled cucumber

1 cup thinly sliced peeled tomato

1 cup salad greens cut crosswise into 1/2-inch strips

1 tbsp plain yogurt

Ground black pepper, dill and mayonnaise to taste

Method:

In a salad bowl, stir all ingredients.

Price for 4 servings:

Corn	$0.80
Cauliflower	$0.50
Tomato	$0.10
Cucumber	$0.10
Salad greens	$0.30
Dressing	$0.10
Total:	$1.90

Day 11

Main dish: Fettuccine Alfredo

Serves 4

Ingredients:

1lb fettuccine noodles, boiled in salted water

1 stick margarine or butter, softened

1 cup grated Parmesan, or other cheese

4 tbsp heavy cream

1 egg yolk

Salt, ground black pepper to taste

Method:

Beat the butter until fluffy. Beat the egg yolk and heavy cream.

When well blended, beat in cheese, salt, black pepper.

Drain fettuccine well, toss with sauce and serve immediately.

Price for 4 servings:

Noodles	$1.80
Margarine or butter	$0.50
Cheese	$1.60
Cream	$0.20
Yolk	$0.10
Salt, pepper	$0.10
Total:	$4.30

Day 12

Salad: Salad with carrot and cauliflower

Serves 4

Ingredients:

1/2 lb peeled and shredded carrot

1/2 lb boiled in salted water cauliflower, cut into small florets, cool to room temperature

1/2 cup finely chopped fresh parsley

1 tbsp white vinegar

1 tbsp vegetable oil

Ground black pepper, salt to taste

Method:

For dressing: Mix vinegar, vegetable oil, and salt.

For salad: In a salad bowl, stir carrot and parsley with 1/2 part of dressing. In the second bowl, stir cauliflower with a dressing and season with pepper. Divide the carrot and cauliflower among 4 individual plates. Place carrot, then cauliflower in a plate.

Price for 4 servings:

Carrot	$0.50
Cauliflower	$0.50
Parsley	$0.20
Dressing	$0.20
Total:	$1.40

Day 12

Main dish: Rice with Mushrooms

Serves 4

Ingredients:

4 cups cooked in beef stock rice

2/3 lb fresh mushrooms, washed, dried, and thin sliced

1 stick margarine or butter

1 tbsp lemon juice

3 tbsp chopped parsley

1/2 cup chopped onion

Method:

Spray mushrooms with lemon juice.

Melt margarine in a saucepan. Add mushrooms, onion, and sauté for 5 minutes. Add mushrooms, onion, and parsley to the hot rice. Stir well, and serve immediately.

Price for 4 servings:

Rice	$1.20
Margarine or butter	$0.50
Mushrooms	$1.60
Beef stock	$0.70
Lemon juice	$0.10
Onion	$0.10
Parsley	$0.10
Total:	$4.30

Day 13

Salad: Red salad

Serves 4

Ingredients:

1/2 lb of shredded red cabbage

1 medium red onion, thinly sliced

1 bunch of radishes, sliced

1 bunch of red-leaf salad

For dressing:

1 garlic clove, peeled and minced

2 tbsp vegetable oil

1 tbsp vinegar

1 tsp French mustard

1 tsp honey

Salt, ground black pepper to taste

Method:

For dressing: Combine all of the dressing ingredients in a bowl. Whisk together thoroughly.

For salad: In a salad bowl, combine the cabbage and dressing. Set aside for 15 minutes. Add radishes, onion and torn salad leaves to the bowl, stir well.

Price for 4 servings:

Cabbage	$0.40
Radishes	$0.50
Red-leaf salad	$0.60
Onion	$0.10
Dressing	$0.40
Total:	$2.00

Day 13

Main dish: Chicken in lemon-dill sauce

Serves 4

Ingredients:

1 frying chicken cut into serving pieces

4 champignons, washed, drained and sliced

1 stick margarine

1 clove garlic, minced

2 tbsp lemon juice

2 tbsp dill, finely chopped

1 tsp paprika

Salt, pepper, Dash to taste

Garnish

Method:

Melt margarine in a large, non-stick skillet; add all ingredients (except chicken), bring to boil. Add chicken, cover the skillet, and lower the heat. Simmer for about 30 minutes; serve with rice, potato, or noodles.

Price for 4 servings:

Chicken	$3.50
Mushrooms	$0.30
Margarine	$0.20
Garlic	$0.10
Spices	$0.40
Garnish	$0.50
Total:	$5.00

Day 14

Salad: Fresh salad with celery and apple

Serves 4

Ingredients:

1 celery root, shredded (or 3 celery stalks, thinly sliced)

4 peeled, seeded and chopped apples

3 tbsp light sour cream or yogurt

1 tbsp horseradish of cream style

Salt, sugar, greens to taste

Method:

In a large salad bowl, combine all ingredients and stir well.

Price for 4 servings:

Celery	$0.50
Apples	$0.50
Dressing	$0.50
Total:	$1.50

Day 14

Main dish: Salmon steaks in foil

Serves 4

Ingredients:

4 salmon fillets (1 lb)

1 lemon

1 tbsp fish seasoning mix (dry onion, garlic, parsley, pepper, etc.)

Salt, pepper to taste

Garnish

Method:

Preheat oven to 375 degrees F. Place every fillet on a piece of cooking foil. Pour lemon juice, sprinkle with seasoning mix; seal each parcel, then bake in oven for about 25 minutes. Serve with fried or baked potato, rice, or noodles.

Price for 4 servings:

Salmon	$4.00
Lemon	$0.30
Spices	$0.20
Garnish	$0.50
Total:	$5.00

Day 15

Salad: Coleslaw

Serves 8

Ingredients:

For salad:

3 cup of green cabbage, shredded

3 cup of red cabbage, shredded

3 stalks celery, chopped

1 bunch radishes, sliced

1 carrot, peeled and grated

1/2 onion chopped

1 green bell pepper, chopped

1 red bell pepper, chopped

For dressing:

3 tbsp mayonnaise

3 tbsp vegetable oil

1 tbsp white wine or white vinegar

Method:

Combine cabbages, celery, radish, carrot, onion and bell peppers in a large bowl, then toss until combined. Combine the dressing ingredients, stir well, pour over salad and mix well.

Price for 8 servings:

Celery	$0.10
Green cabbage	$0.20
Red cabbage	$0.30
Radishes	$0.50
Red bell pepper	$0.60
Green bell pepper	$0.50
Carrot	$0.20
Onion	$0.10
Dressing	$0.30
Total:	$2.80

Day 15

Main dish: Orange beef

Serves 4

Ingredients:

1 lb beef, cut into thin strips

1/2 cup cornstarch

1 onion, thinly sliced

1 green bell pepper, seeded, and cut into strips

2 tbsp soy sauce, 1/3 cup sugar, 1/3 cup cold water

2 tbsp vegetable oil

4 cups cooked rice

Other seasoning to taste

Method:

Mix water, sugar, soy sauce, and 3 tbsp cornstarch well, then set aside. Heat oil in a large skillet, and place the meat-coated cornstarch onto the skillet. Stir-fry the beef until brown on both sides, add vegetables, and stir-fry for about 2 minutes. Add the seasoning mixture, then stir-fry until thickened (about 3-4 minutes). Serve with cooked rice.

Price for 4 servings:

Meat	$2.50
Bell pepper	$0.50
Onion	$0.10
Cornstarch	$0.20
Soy sauce, sugar	$0.20
Vegetable oil	$0.10
Rice	$0.50
Total:	$4.10

Day 16

Salad: Salad with spinach and buttermilk

Serves 4

Ingredients:

1/2 pound fresh spinach, washed and cut into thin stripes

1 bunch of green onions, thinly sliced

For dressing: 1 cup buttermilk

1 tbsp vegetable oil

1/2 cup parsley, chopped

2 tsp lemon juice

1 hard-cooked egg, grated

Salt, ground black pepper to taste

Method:

For dressing: Combine all of the dressing ingredients in a bowl. Whisk together thoroughly.

For salad: In a salad bowl, combine the spinach, green onions and dressing. Stir well.

Price for 4 servings:

Spinach	$0.20
Green onions	$0.50
Buttermilk	$0.40
Parsley	$0.20
Egg	$0.10
Lemon juice	$0.10
Spices	$0.10
Total:	$1.60

Day 16

Main dish: Spaghetti with tomato-mushroom sauce

Serves 4

Ingredients:

3 cup mushrooms, sliced

1/4 cup all-purpose flour

1/4 cup butter or margarine, 3 cup milk

1/2 cup Parmesan cheese, grated

1 medium onion, chopped

1 tbsp vegetable oil

3 tbsp tomato sauce

1 lb spaghetti, uncooked

Salt, pepper, chopped fresh parsley to taste

Method:

Melt butter in a saucepan over medium heat. Stir in flour and cook for 1 minute. Add milk, salt and pepper and stir vigorously. Whip until mixture barely comes to a boil. Reduce heat and simmer for 5 minutes, whipping frequently while the sauce thickens. Keep warm. Heat vegetable oil in a large skillet over medium heat. Add sliced mushrooms and minced onions, sauté until onion is golden, then add tomato sauce, stir well and sauté for about 5 minutes. Add to the sauce. Meanwhile, cook spaghetti according to the package directions. Drain well and add to the sauce along with the parsley. Blend well and transfer to serving dish. Sprinkle with Parmesan cheese and serve immediately.

Price for 4 servings:

Mushrooms	$2.90
Onion	$0.10
Margarine	$0.20
Milk	$0.50
Cheese	$0.40
Spaghetti	$0.70
Spices, sauce, flour	$0.20
Total:	$5.00

Day 17

Salad: Greek salad

Serves 4

Ingredients:

1/2 head of lettuce, torn or cut

1 tomato, cut into wedges

1/2 peeled and sliced cucumber

1/2 sweet onion, thinly sliced

1 green bell pepper, seeded and sliced

1 cup cheese, cut into small cubes

1 cup black olives (optional)

2 tbsp vegetable oil

1 tbsp lemon juice

Greens to taste

Method:

Combine in a salad bowl all vegetables; toss to mix.

Add to bowl cheese and olives. Combine vegetable oil, lemon juice, and greens. Pour the dressing over the vegetables and cheese.

Price for 4 servings:

Lettuce	$0.40
Green bell pepper	$0.50
Onion	$0.10
Tomato	$0.30
Cucumber	$0.30
Cheese	$0.80
Dressing	$0.10
Total:	$2.50

Day 17

Main dish: Grilled Chicken Breast Tenders

Serves 4

Ingredients:

1 lb chicken breast tenders

1/2 cup Italian dressing (drain and discard spices)

1 tsp fresh lemon (or lime) juice

1 1/2 tsp honey

Method:

Mix dressing, lime juice and honey together. Pour over chicken tenders, making sure all the tenders are covered. Marinate for 1/2 hour. Braise tenders in a non-stick pan or grill until lightly golden colored but not dry. Serve with noodles, potatoes, or rice.

Price for 4 servings:

Chicken breasts	$2.90
Lemon juice	$0.20
Honey	$0.50
Dressing	$0.10
Garnish	$0.50
Total:	$4.20

Day 18

Salad: Salad with beet and walnuts

Serves 4

Ingredients:

1 large beet, roasted until tender (about 35 minutes), cooled, peeled and shredded

2 apples, peeled, seeded and shredded

1/2 cup walnuts, grated

Washed raisins and light mayonnaise to taste

Method:

Combine all the ingredients in a salad bowl. Stir well.

Price for 4 servings:

Beet	$0.60
Apples	$0.30
Walnuts	$1.00
Dressing	$0.10
Total:	$2.00

Day 18

Main dish: Mushroom Soufflé

Serves 4

Ingredients:

4 cups fresh mushrooms, washed, dried, and finely chopped

3 tbsp margarine or butter

5 tbsp all-purpose flour

1 cup milk

1/2 cup red wine

5 eggs, separated

Salt, pepper to taste

Method:

Toss mushrooms with lemon juice.

Combine milk, red wine, and mushrooms in saucepan, bring to boil, then reduce heat, and simmer for 10 minutes. Melt the butter in a saucepan, stir in flour, and cook, stirring constantly, until golden (about 4 minutes). Stir in mushroom mixture; cook for 3 minutes, stirring constantly. Beat egg yolks, add slowly into the mushroom mixture. Beat well. Bring to almost boiling but do not boil, then remove from heat. Stir until cooled, and then add whipped egg whites. Add butter and flour casserole, then place the mushroom mixture in the casserole.

Bake in preheated 350 degrees F oven until puffed, brown, and firm in the center. Serve immediately.

Price for 4 servings:

Milk	$0.30
Margarine or butter	$0.40
Mushrooms	$2.00
Red wine	$0.70
Eggs	$0.50
Salt, pepper	$0.10
Total:	$4.00

Day 19

Salad: Summer salad

Serves 4

Ingredients:

For salad:

4 medium zucchini, peeled and cut into cubes

For dressing:

1/2-cup buttermilk

2 tablespoons vegetable oil

2 tablespoons chopped fresh parsley

1 teaspoon lemon juice

3 to 4 cloves garlic, crushed

Salt to taste

Method:

Toss zucchini with enough flour to coat. In a large nonstick frying pan, heat 1 tablespoon of the oil over moderate heat. Add the zucchini and cook, stirring occasionally, for about 15 minutes, until the vegetables begin to feel tender when pierced with a knife or a skewer. Let cool. Whip the buttermilk with 1 tbsp of vegetable oil, garlic, lemon juice and parsley. In a salad bowl, combine the zucchini and dressing, then stir well.

Price for 4 servings:

Flour	$0.10
Zucchini	$1.30
Dressing	$0.50
Total:	$1.90

Day 19

Main dish: Chicken Meatballs with Rice

Serves 4

Ingredients:

1 lb ground chicken

2 cup cooked rice

1 medium onion, chopped

4 tbsp light sour cream

Salt and spices to taste

Method:

In a bowl, combine ground chicken, rice, chopped onion, salt and spices. Stir well.

In a large saucepan, combine water, salt, and spices, and bring to boil. Shape round meatballs with wet hands, then place them in a saucepan. Cook until ready, or for about 12-15 minutes over medium heat, then remove meatballs with a slotted spoon. Arrange on a serving platter, spoon sour cream over meatballs. Serve immediately.

Price for 4 servings:

Ground chicken	$2.50
Rice	$0.50
Onion	$0.20
Sour cream	$0.50
Salt, pepper	$0.10
Total:	$3.70

Day 20

Salad: German vegetable salad

Serves 4

Ingredients:

1 medium beet, baked until tender, about 35 minutes, cooled, peeled and shredded

1 large potato, baked until tender, cooled, peeled and cut into cubes

1 apple, peeled, seeded and shredded

1/2 onion, fine chopped

1 marinated cucumber, fine chopped

1 tbsp vegetable oil

Salt, vinegar, fresh chopped parsley to taste

Washed raisins and mayonnaise to taste

Method:

In a salad bowl, combine all the ingredients; stir well.

Price for 4 servings:

Beet	$0.40
Potato	$0.20
Onion	$0.10
Apple	$0.20
Cucumber	$0.10
Raisings	$0.4 0
Dressing	$0.30
Total:	$1.70

Day 20

Main dish: Meatballs

Serves 4

Ingredients:

1/2 lb ground beef

1/2 lb ground pork

3 fresh eggs

1 cup milk

1/4 dried Sourdough bread, or hard

1 large onion, finely chopped

2 tbsp vegetable oil

1 tbsp sour cream

1 tsp salt

Spices to taste

Method:

Pour milk in a large bowl; soak bread in milk for about 10 minutes. Add beef, pork, onion, salt, eggs, and the seasoning into the bowl and mix very well. Heat oil in a large skillet. Shape the meat mixture into balls of about 2 inches in diameter. In a large saucepan, bring the broth, ground pepper, salt, and your favorite spices to boil. Then, lower heat, add sour cream, and simmer the meatballs for about 20 minutes. Serve with noodles, potato, or rice; pour with stock.

Price for 4 servings:

Ground meat	$2.70
Eggs	$0.30
Onion	$0.30
Milk	$0.10
Bread	$0.30
Spices	$0.10
Vegetable oil	$0.10
Garnish	$0.50
Total:	$4.40

Day 21

Salad: Fresh salad with cabbage and carrot

Serves 4

Ingredients:

1/2 lb cabbage, shredded

2 carrots, peeled and shredded

Soft cream cheese to taste

1-2 tbsp vegetable oil

Method:

Combine all the ingredients in a salad bowl and mix together thoroughly.

Price for 4 servings:

Cabbage	$0.30
Carrot	$0.40
Cream cheese	$1.00
Vegetable oil	$0.10
Total:	$1.80

Day 21

Main dish: Sweet and Sour Pork

Serves 4

Ingredients:

1 lb non-fat pork, sliced into 1 inch x 2 inch stripes, thick not more than 1/2 inch

5 tbsp cornstarch or potato starch

1 large onion, thinly sliced

1 medium tomato, peeled and cut into cubes

1 green bell pepper, seeded and sliced

3 tsp sugar, 3 tsp ketchup, ½ cup water, 1/3 cup soy sauce, 2 tsp vegetable oil

Method:

In a mixing bowl, combine pork and 3 tbsp cornstarch. Mix to coat. In a small mixing bowl, whisk water, vegetable oil, 3 tbsp cornstarch, ketchup, and soy sauce. Heat the oil in large skillet.

Add pork and stir-fry until brown, remove by a slotted spoon and dry using paper towels.

Add the onion, bell pepper and tomato to the skillet. Add 1 tbsp water, and stir-fry for 2 minutes. Add the soy sauce mixture and pork; simmer for 5 minutes or until the sauce thickens. Stir and serve over cooked rice or cooked noodles.

Note: Additionally, you can use other vegetables: julienne-cut carrot, green peas, broccoli, pineapple chunks, etc. You can use chicken or beef instead pork.

Price for 4 servings:

Meat	$2.70
Tomato	$0.20
Onion	$0.30
Soy sauce	$0.30
Bell pepper	$0.60
Sauce mix	$0.30
Vegetable oil	$0.10
Garnish	$0.50
Total:	$5.00

Day 22

Salad: Fresh salad with cabbage, carrot and apple

Serves 4

Ingredients:

1/2 lb cabbage, shredded

2 carrots, peeled and shredded

2 apple, peeled, seeded and cut into small cubes

1/2 cup olives, thinly sliced

1 cup plain yogurt

1-2 tbsp vegetable oil

Method:

Combine all the ingredients in a salad bowl; mix together.

Price for 4 servings:

Cabbage	$0.30
Carrots	$0.40
Olives	$0.30
Apple	$0.30
Garden greens	$0.30
Yogurt	$0.30
Total:	$1.90

Day 22

Main dish: Fish and Rice Bake

Serves 4

Ingredients:

1 lb cheapest fish fillets, thawed

3 cups hot cooked rice

2 tbsp margarine, melted

1 egg, beaten

1 onion, chopped

1 tbsp lemon juice, 1/2 tsp salt, paprika to taste

Method:

Cut the fish into 1-inch pieces. Combine rice, egg, salt, and onion; spread it into an even layer in the oven-safe dish. Top with fish pieces. Drizzle with melted margarine, lemon juice and salt. Cover with foil.

Bake in a 350 degrees F oven 25 minutes, then uncover and bake for 5-7 minutes.

Price for 4 servings:

Fish	$3.90
Egg	$0.10
Onion	$0.20
Spices	$0.20
Margarine	$0.10
Rice	$0.50
Total:	$5.00

Day 23

Salad: Favorite Gete's salad

Serves 4

Ingredients:

1 bunch cress-salad, washed and thinly sliced

2 cup spinach or sorrel, washed and thinly sliced

1 cup of mixed garden greens (dill, green onion, parsley), finely chopped

1 cup buttermilk

Salt, pepper, lemon or lime juice to taste

Method:

In a salad bowl, mix cress salad, spinach and garden greens.

In a small bowl, combine buttermilk, spices and lime juice. Whisk together thoroughly. Add to the salad bowl and stir well.

Price for 4 servings:

Cress salad	$0.40
Spinach	$0.20
Garden greens	$0.10
Buttermilk	$0.20
Dressing	$0.30
Total:	$1.70

Day 23

Main dish: Shrimp Risotto

Serves 4

Ingredients:

1 lb shrimp

For stock:

2 cups uncooked rice

1 medium onion, sliced, 1 stalk celery, chopped, 1 clove garlic

1 cup mushrooms, sliced

1 green bell pepper

1 package frozen peas, thawed

1 tbsp red vinegar, 3 cups water

Method:

Combine hot water, rice, onion, and vinegar in a large saucepan; bring to boil, then simmer gently 10 minutes.

Add mushrooms, celery, peas, and green pepper. Cover and simmer for 10 minutes. Add shrimp and boil for 3-5 minutes,

Serve immediately.

Price for 4 servings:

Shrimps	$3.00
Peas	$0.60
Onion, celery, garlic	$0.20
Bell pepper	$0.60
Vinegar	$0.10
Rice	$0.50
Total:	$5.00

Day 24

Salad: Cheese salad

Serves 4

Ingredients:

2 tomato, peeled, seeded and sliced

3 apple, peeled, seeded and sliced

1 sweet onion, shredded, blanched about 1 minute and drained

1 cup soft cream cheese

Sugar, salt and other spices to taste

Method:

Combine all the ingredients in a salad bowl; stir very well.

Price for 4 servings:

Tomato	$0.40
Apple	$0.40
Onion	$0.10
Cream cheese	$0.90
Total:	$1.80

Day 24

Main dish: Yankee Doodle Macaroni

Serves 4

Ingredients:

1 package macaroni, cooked in boiled water and drained well

1 lb ground beef

1 lb peeled tomatoes

1/2 cup sliced mushrooms

1 large onion, finely chopped

2 cloves garlic, minced

3 tbsp margarine

Salt, pepper, chopped parsley, grated cheese to taste

Method:

Toss the macaroni in 2 tbsp of margarine, then set aside. Keep hot.

In a large pan, heat margarine, then add onion, garlic, and mushrooms.

Sauté until onion just brown, then add meat. Stir until the meat is brown, add tomatoes and seasoning. Cover, and simmer for 20-30 minutes, then pour this sauce over the macaroni, and sprinkle with grated cheese. Serve immediately.

Note: You can use any other kind of noodles and any other pasta sauce.

Price for 4 servings:

Macaroni	$0.80
Margarine	$0.20
Cheese	$0.50
Tomatoes	$0.90
Ground meat	$2.50
Salt, pepper, parsley	$0.10
Total:	$5.00

Day 25

Salad: Salad with potato and tomato

Serves 4

Ingredients:

  2 tomatoes, peeled, seeded and sliced

  3 potatoes, peeled, broiled until ready and cut

  1 sweet onion, shredded

  2 hard-cook eggs

  3 celery stalks

  4 tbsp any vinaigrette

  Sugar, salt and other spices to taste

Method:

  Mix all the ingredients in a salad bowl.

Price for 4 servings:

Tomato	$0.40
Potato	$0.20
Onion	$0.20
Eggs	$0.30
Celery	$0.40
Vinaigrette	$0.30
Total:	$1.70

Day 25

Main dish: Spinach and Mushroom Soufflé

Serves 4

Ingredients:

1 bunch of spinach

1 cup mushrooms, sliced

1 garlic clove, crushed

1 cup milk

½ stick margarine, melted

3 tbsp all-purpose flour

6 fresh eggs, separated

Salt, freshly ground black pepper

Method:

Steam the spinach 3-5 minutes, cool under running water, then drain, then chop finely. In a saucepan cook the garlic and mushrooms with the margarine until softened and juices evaporated.

In a blender, stir the flour, 3 tbsp the cold milk and egg yolks, blend well. Bring to boil remained milk, then

Stir the boiling milk into the egg-flour mix, place to pan and simmer over moderate heat until to thicken. Then add chopped spinach, garlic and mushrooms, salt and black pepper to pan, stir with whipped egg whites. Butter a soufflé dish and add mixture into the dish. Bake in the oven for about 25 minutes, until puffed and golden brown. Serve immediately.

Price for 4 servings:

Spinach	$0.90
Egg	$0.60
Onion	$0.20
Mushrooms	$1.60
Margarine	$0.30
Flour	$0.10
Spices	$0.10
Total:	$3.80

Day 26

Salad: Summer vinaigrette

Serves 4

Ingredients:

1 medium beet, boiled until ready, peeled and cut

2 potatoes, peeled, boiled until ready and cut

1 carrot, broiled until ready, peeled and cut

1/2-lb boiled in salted water cauliflower, cut into small florets

1 hard-cook egg, shredded

1 cup fresh green peas

4 leaves any salad greens

1/2 cup plain yogurt or light sour cream

1 tbsp dill, finely chopped

Method:

Mix all the ingredients, except of salad greens, in a salad bowl. Place on plate leaf of salad greens. Place salad over the salad greens.

Price for 4 servings:

Beet	$0.40
Cauliflower	$0.50
Potato	$0.20
Carrot	$0.20
Egg	$0.10
Salad greens	$0.20
Green peas	$0.20
Dressing	$0.20
Total:	$2.00

Day 26

Main dish: Mushroom Bolognese

Serves 4

Ingredients:

1 lb champignons, washed, dried and cut into quarters

1 medium onion, chopped

1 garlic clove, crushed

1 tbsp tomato paste

1 medium tomato, peeled and chopped

1 tbsp vegetable oil

1 tbsp oregano, chopped

1 lb cooked hot pasta

3 tbsp grated cheese

Method:

Heat the oil in a large pan, add onions and garlic and cook for 2-3 minutes. Add the mushrooms to the pan, cook for 3-4 minutes over high heat, stirring occasionally. Stir in tomato, tomato pasta and oregano. Lower the heat, cover and cook for 5 minutes. Add salt and pepper, mix. In a mixing bowl, combine pasta and sauce, toss well and serve immediately, topped with grated cheese.

Price for 4 servings:

Pasta	$0.80
Mushrooms	$3.00
Cheese	$0.30
Tomato and tomato pasta	$0.30
Onion	$0.20
Garlic	$0.10
Salt, pepper, oregano	$0.20
Vegetable oil	$0.10
Total:	$5.00

Day 27

Salad: Fresh salad with tomato and egg

Serves 4

Ingredients:

4 tomatoes, peeled and cut

1 hard-cook egg, shredded

4 leaves any salad greens

1/2 cup plain yogurt or light sour cream

1 tbsp dill or parsley, finely chopped

Seasoning to taste

Method:

Mix all the ingredients, except of salad greens, in a salad bowl. Place on plate leaf of salad greens. Place salad over the salad greens.

Price for 4 servings:

Tomatoes	$0.90
Egg	$0.10
Salad greens	$0.20
Greens	$0.10
Dressing	$0.20
Total:	$1.50

Day 27

Main dish: Vegetable Mix with Milk Sauce

Serves 4

Ingredients:

2 lb mixture of vegetables, peeled and cut

2 tbsp all-purpose flour

1/4 cup butter or margarine, melted

2 cup hot milk

1 qt water

Salt and other spices to taste

Method:

Pour salted water in a pan, and bring to boil. Add vegetable mixture, and boil until ready. Drain and set aside.

Heat margarine in a saucepan over medium heat. Stir in flour and cook for about 1 minute. Add hot milk and salt, then stir vigorously with a wire whip just until the mixture comes to a boil. Reduce heat and simmer for 10-15 minutes, whipping frequently while the sauce thickens. Sprinkle spices to taste. Pour sauce over the vegetables. Toss well, and transfer to the serving dish.

Price for 4 servings:

Vegetables	$3.00
Milk	$0.30
Margarine	$0.20
Flour	$0.10
Spices	$0.10
Total:	$3.70

Day 28

Salad: Fresh salad with cabbage and egg

Serves 4

Ingredients:

1 lb cabbage, shredded

2 hard-cook eggs, grated

1/2 sweet onion, finely chopped

2 tbsp vegetable oil

Salt to taste

Method:

In a salad bowl, mix the cabbage and salt, then knead by hands until juicy (about 5 minutes).

Add eggs and vegetable oil to a bowl, and mix everything together.

Price for 4 servings:

Cabbage	$0.80
Eggs	$0.30
Onion	$0.10
Vegetable oil	$0.10
Total:	$1.30

Day 28

Main dish: Cheese and Potato Patties

Serves 4

Ingredients:

2 lb potato

1/2 lb cottage cheese or shredded cheese

1 egg, beaten

1 medium onion, chopped

2 tbsp all-purpose flour

3 tbsp vegetable oil

3 tbsp chopped fresh dill, or 1 tbsp dried dill

Salt, ground black pepper to taste

Method:

Boil the potatoes in their skins until soft, then drain and peel. Place into a bowl, and mash. Mix with the cottage cheese, egg, onion, dill, salt and black pepper. Chill the mixture, and then divide it into walnut-sized balls. Flatten them slightly and coat with flour.

Heat the oil in the frying pan. Fry the patties until golden or golden brown on each side. Drain using paper towels, and serve.

Price for 4 servings:

Potato	$0.90
Egg	$0.10
Onion	$0.10
Vegetable oil	$0.10
Flour	$0.10
Cottage cheese	$1.50
Dill	$0.80
Salt, pepper	$0.10
Total:	$3.70

Day 29

Salad: Fresh salad with Daikon radish, carrot and apple
Serves 4

Ingredients:

1/2 lb Daikon radish, peeled and grated

2 carrots, peeled and grated

2 apple, peeled, seeded and grated

2 cup green cabbage, shredded

For dressing:

2 tbsp vegetable oil

1 tsp lemon juice

2 tbsp parsley, finely chopped

Sugar, salt, pepper to taste

Method:

In a small bowl, combine the dressing ingredients and mix well.

In a salad bowl, combine all the vegetables and stir well.

Price for 4 servings:

Cabbage	$0.20
Carrot	$0.40
Daikon	$0.50
Apple	$0.30
Dressing	$0.30
Total:	$1.70

Day 29

Main dish: Mix meat patties

Serves 4

Ingredients:

1/2 lb ground beef

1/2 lb ground pork

3 fresh eggs

1 cup milk

1/4 dry Sourdough bread

1 large onion, finely chopped

2 tbsp vegetable oil

1 tbsp sour cream

1 tsp salt

Spices to taste

Method:

Pour milk in a large bowl, add bread, and knead. Add the beef, pork, onion, salt, eggs and seasoning into the bowl, and mix very well. Heat oil in a large skillet. Shape patties as desired. Cook until both sides are brown. Then, pour hot water and sour cream into the skillet. Cover, and simmer patties for about 20 minutes. Serve with noodles, potatoes, or rice.

Price for 4 servings:

Ground meat	$2.70
Eggs	$0.30
Onion	$0.30
Milk	$0.10
Bread	$0.30
Spices	$0.10
Vegetable oil	$0.10
Garnish	$0.50
Total:	$4.40

Day 30

Salad: Fresh salad with cress salad, onion and egg

Serves 4

Ingredients:

4 cups cress salad, washed, drained and thinly sliced

2 hard-cook eggs, grated

1 bunch green onions, washed, drained and thinly sliced

2 tbsp vegetable oil

1/2 cup light sour cream or plain yogurt

Salt to taste

Method:

In a salad bowl, combine all the ingredients and stir well.

Remark: You can use another kind of salad and another dressing. Feel free to add your favorite greens.

Price for 4 servings:

Cress salad	$0.80
Green onions	$0.50
Eggs	$0.20
Dressing	$0.30
Total:	$1.80

Day 30

Main dish: Fish fillets in dill sauce

Serves 4

Ingredients:

1 lb catfish (or other fish) fillets

1 tbsp lemon juice

1 large onion, finely chopped

1 cup milk

3 tbsp all-purpose flour

1 tbsp dill, finely chopped

Garnish

Method:

Season the fillets to taste with salt and pepper, then sprinkle with lemon juice. Heat the oil in a skillet, add fish, and brown well (about 10 minutes on each side).

Remove fillets, add onion, and cook until golden. Heat a medium sized skillet, add flour and cook, stirring constantly until golden. Then, pour milk, stirring thoroughly. Bring to boil, but do not boil. Stir in a chopped onion, remove from heat, and stir in chopped dill. Serve with rice, potato, and noodles. Place garnish on the plate, and place fillet on top of the garnish. Then, pour dill sauce over the fish.

Price for 4 servings:

Fish fillets	$3.60
Flour	$0.10
Onion	$0.20
Milk	$0.10
Lemon juice	$0.10
Dill	$0.20
Vegetable oil	$0.10
Garnish	$0.50
Total:	$4.90

Day 31

Salad: Fresh salad with Daikon Radish and carrot

Serves 4

Ingredients:

  2 carrots, peeled and cut into long, thin strips

  1 small Daikon radish or turnip, peeled and cut into long, thin strips

  1 tbsp shopped parsley

  For dressing:

  3 tbsp rice vinegar

  2 tsp sugar

  1/4 tsp sea salt

  1 tsp sesame oil

  2 tsp vegetable oil

Method:

Prepare dressing: pour vinegar, sugar, salt and oils. Stir until sugar and salt dissolve then set aside. Squeeze excess moisture from the carrots and turnips. Place the carrots and turnips into a salad bowl and toss with dressing. Marinate for at least 10 minutes. Add the parsley on top. Chill until served.

Price for 4 servings:

Carrot	$0.40
Daikon	$0.50
Parsley	$0.10
Dressing	$0.70
Total:	$1.70

Day 31

Main dish: Ginger beef

Serves 4

Ingredients:

1 lb beef, cut into small cubes, or into thin strips

1/2 lb fresh tomatoes, peeled and diced

1 large onion, finely chopped

2 gloves garlic, pressed

2 tsp ginger

1 tsp chili powder (optional)

2 tbsp vegetable oil

4 cups cooked rice

1/2 cup hot water

Salt, pepper, other seasoning to taste

Method:

Heat the oil in a large skillet, place meat, onion, and garlic into the skillet. Stir-fry the beef until browned on all sides, add ginger, chili powder, and tomatoes. Stir well. Add water, stir well. Cook for about 5 minutes, stirring constantly. Serve with cooked rice.

Price for 4 servings:

Meat	$3.00
Tomato	$0.50
Onion	$0.30
Garlic	$0.20
Spices	$0.40
Vegetable oil	$0.10
Rice	$0.50
Total:	$5.00

0-595-25916-2

www.ingramcontent.com/pod-product-compliance
Lightning Source LLC
Chambersburg PA
CBHW030742180526
45163CB00003B/886